From Seed to Sapling:

How God Turned a Seed of Vision Into a Tree of Life

By Adam Sterenberg, Founder of Schools of Life -Tree of Life

Foreword by John Booy, A Founder of The Potter's
House in Grand Rapids, Michigan

FROM SEED TO SAPLING

*How God Turned a Seed of
Vision Into a Tree of Life*

ADAM STERENBERG

WESTBOW·
PRESS
A DIVISION OF THOMAS NELSON
& ZONDERVAN

Edited by Sonya Bernard-Hollins, Season Press LLC, Kalamazoo, Michigan

Scripture quotations marked (NLT) are taken from the Holy Bible, New Living Translation, copyright © 1996, 2004, 2007 by Tyndale House Foundation. Used by permission of Tyndale House Publishers, Inc., Carol Stream, Illinois 60188. All rights reserved.

*Note to Readers: This book contains some of the many stories of students, business leaders and volunteers who helped contribute to the story of Tree of Life. Some of the names have been changed to protect the identity of those who wish to remain anonymous. Many of their personal notes have not been edited to remain true to the author's voice.

For information visit:
Tree of Life School – www.tolschool.org
River of Life School- www.riveroflifeschool.org
Proceeds from the sale of this book go to support Tree of Life Schools.

WestBow Press books may be ordered through booksellers or by contacting:

WestBow Press
A Division of Thomas Nelson & Zondervan
1663 Liberty Drive
Bloomington, IN 47403
www.westbowpress.com
1 (866) 928-1240

Because of the dynamic nature of the Internet, any web addresses or links contained in this book may have changed since publication and may no longer be valid. The views expressed in this work are solely those of the author and do not necessarily reflect the views of the publisher, and the publisher hereby disclaims any responsibility for them.

Any people depicted in stock imagery provided by Thinkstock are models, and such images are being used for illustrative purposes only.
Certain stock imagery © Thinkstock.

ISBN: 978-1-4908-5646-9 (sc)
ISBN: 978-1-4908-5648-3 (hc)
ISBN: 978-1-4908-5647-6 (e)

Library of Congress Control Number: 2014918405

Printed in the United States of America.

WestBow Press rev. date: 11/06/2014

CONTENTS

This book was written for the glory of our King and dedicated to all of you who move in faith and realize the price of obedience is worth it all.
A.S.

Thanks
I thank God.
I thank everyone involved.
I thank everyone who has helped.
He is the Head and we are the Body.

FOREWORD

People often ask if the whole concept of Christ-centered schools for the urban child is realistic. Are they affordable? Are they sustainable? Is it *possible* to offer an excellent, rigorous, Christ-centered education to the impoverished youth of our cities across the nation? To this, I oftentimes answer, if there's a God and He is who He says He is, then not only *is* it possible, but it *must* be possible.

Throughout scripture, God clearly states that His heart goes out to the marginalized, to the widow, to the orphan and to the alien in our midst. The only way Christ-centered schools would be available *only* to the rich would be if God were an illusion. But, if at the center of this universe is the communal Trinity of the Father, Son and Holy Spirit––eternally in love with each other and giving to each other and inviting others to enter into that "community of love" ––then, not only is it possible that Christ-centered schools can exist, but they *must* exist because that's who our God is.

Adam Sterenberg and the Tree of Life School's staff have vision and confidence. It's that confidence in the character of God that enables them to risk everything–their reputations, their nice homes in the suburbs, their salaries, and their security––for this dream of offering an excellent Christ-centered education to the children of Kalamazoo.

The Potter's House School in Grand Rapids, Michigan (about fifty miles from Kalamazoo) started in much the same way. We were a group of people who felt God was calling us to move into the southwest side of Grand Rapids and quit our jobs in order to provide Christ-centered education for those formerly without access. Now, thirty-three years later, we have 569 students we help educate by raising $3.4 million a year! With only 20% of our operational cost based on tuition provided by the students, we have to rely completely on God to provide the 80% each year. God has proved himself faithful year after year. All of our bills are paid. We pretty much finish each year in the black.

Even with that history of God's faithfulness I have to say that I have been deeply challenged by the radical faith of Adam. When we started the Potter's House we were fresh out of college and living in a community of people who shared the resources. It was fairly easy to say we'd quit our jobs to teach for free. Adam's story is of a deeper faith. He had a family, a well-established job, and a nice home in the suburbs, and he was willing to risk all of that to follow after God's call. Adam is a man who completely relies on the Holy Spirit.

He listens to the Spirit's promptings, and he follows in obedience. He does it in a community of people who are committed to each other to live out this Kingdom call in transparency and accountability to focus on the poor. As you read through these pages of Adam's story, I hope you will be as inspired and challenged as I was.

John Booy,
Superintendent of The Potter's House in Grand Rapids,
Michigan

PROLOGUE

In the Beginning

"What is the mission statement for *your* life?"

That was the question posed to us by Pastor Bob at the Christian Educators Convention. The year was 2003, and I was attending the convention in Milwaukee, Wisconsin with a few of my colleagues from Kalamazoo Christian Schools. We were attending the sectional workshop entitled "Hallways of Grace."

A short time after the workshop began, it seemed to me that everything in the room began to fade away. It was kind of like those old television shows when the screen went wavy during a flashback scene; except, this was no flashback. It's hard to describe, but what I can say is that God spoke to me at that moment. He spoke to my spirit and told me to start a school in the city of Kalamazoo––a Christian school where lack of finances would not deter students from attending.

Years would go by before I began to act on my "calling" from God. I was led to move my family from the suburbs of Kalamazoo into the inner city. We changed churches and would later join one located in a formerly abandoned factory building I noticed a year earlier in our new Edison neighborhood. When I first saw it during our walk through the neighborhood, I asked my wife, "Wouldn't that building be a perfect place for a Christian school?"

Those who prayed with me said they did see a school being built and that I would need help. Destiny began to reveal itself as two other men of God joined in to help make the vision a reality. Then others joined in to unknowingly play a role in something bigger than they could have ever imagined.

In this book, I will do my best to describe the incidents that allowed my vision from God to become a reality. The journey wasn't easy. And, as I look back on the trials, triumphs and miracles that happened along the way, I can't help but realize that God's hands were constantly moving.

Had someone told me the story of how the Tree of Life School was founded, I might find it hard to believe. I would have thought it was a stretch of the imagination at the least. But it happened, and I am a witness of how God can take a vision and turn it into a tree of life.

PART 1

The Seed

*"Then Joshua asked them, 'How long are you going to wait
before taking possession of the remaining land the LORD,
the God of your ancestors, has given to you?'"*
Joshua 18:3

CHAPTER 1

Jesus' Birthday Present

In 2009, I took a bold step and asked God, *Lord, what do you want for your birthday?* It was no surprise when He told me. It was as clear as the first time I truly asked Him a question and heard His voice. What He wanted me to do would not be easy. As far as the world was concerned, I didn't have the training or natural gifting for it.

That's how I know it was from Him. At the time, I didn't realize that He didn't want ME to do anything. What He did want was for me to be obedient, listen to Him and watch Him move mountains. Little did I know He was preparing me for "such a time as this."

My parents, Jim and Kathy Sterenberg, welcomed me into the world in 1971. The Muskegon, Michigan natives loved God and His word and had no problem selecting the name Adam, for their first-born son. A few years later our family grew to include my sister, Rachael. My father worked as a manager for United Parcel Service, which often had him move to other towns as a part of his promotions. The last transfer was within the state from St. Joseph to Kalamazoo, Michigan. I remember the move vividly. I was 12 years old and had to leave some of the best friends of my life.

The Sterenbergs valued education and the safety of their children. They had decided to enroll me into Kalamazoo Christian Schools which had two campuses, South and North Christian elementary schools. North was closer to our house; however, after visiting the neighborhood in which the school was located, my parents opted against it.

They had grown up during the civil rights era and never spoke ill of any ethnic or racial group. North campus was located on Cobb Street, which was mainly occupied by upstanding working-class African Americans. However, those in the neighborhoods surrounding it were no strangers to the crime and violence on their blocks. Because my safety was my parent's number-one priority, it was decided that they would take the extra time to drive me to the South campus on the other side of town.

My spiritual life was going through changes as well. While we had always gone to church, it wasn't until I was 14 years old that I accepted Jesus Christ as my personal Lord, Savior and Friend. After completing a Profession of Faith class I, along with other members of the class, stood in front of the entire church to profess our love for Jesus our Savior.

I went on to graduate from Kalamazoo Christian High School and immediately began my college education at Western Michigan University, which was just across the street from my high school. My goal was to put my love for math and science to good use and become a wealthy architect. I planned to take courses at WMU and after two years transfer to the University of Michigan to complete my degree. God had other plans.

The real challenges began in my sophomore year when I decided to take five challenging classes for a total of seventeen credit hours. More specifically, it was a physics lab class taught by a graduate assistant who began to turn the tide of my plans. She was an international student who barely spoke English. Furthermore, it was painfully obvious to our noses that she did not bathe regularly. One day we asked her for help in completing the wiring for an electrical circuit. As she came to help, we started breathing through our mouths to prevent smelling her. To top it off, she really didn't help us and had no desire to try. I was so stinking mad that I later dropped the class.

My main four-credit physics class was quickly becoming unbearable. I earned 30% on a test and was given a B. Where in the world does 30% equal a B? Other classmates began buying tests from students who had previously taken the class, and I just couldn't keep up. I dropped the class, which took my total credits that semester down to twelve.

As I struggled through my classes, there was growing dissonance inside me that made me feel I would erupt any minute. I couldn't get an architectural internship, and the other jobs didn't seem to pan out. I really started to wonder, *what in the world was going on? What am I here for? Was I headed in the wrong direction?*

One evening, I climbed up into the loft in my dorm room and prayed to God. I asked Him one simple question, "What do *You* want me to be?" The quick and clear response from inside my head was, *a teacher.* Did God really just speak to me? I didn't think He still did that. He didn't want me to move to Africa and become a missionary? Did He really want me to be just a teacher? A wave of shock rolled through my body. I groaned as a memory surfaced from a few weeks before.

> *I was walking on campus by the Faunce Student Center–known by all as the Birdcage because of its distinctive cage-looking roof. My friend, Proehly, talked about how excited she was to become a teacher. As she spoke I realized I no longer had any certainty about being an architect.*
>
> *"You should become a teacher. You'd be good at that," she said to me with much excitement.*
>
> *I chuckled morosely and said, "I think being a teacher would be a big waste of my time and talents."*

I was convicted as I lay in my loft with the lights off. I reflected on that moment from a few weeks ago and decided to switch my major to education. The minute I started education classes I *knew* that's exactly where I was supposed to be. I felt peace. I felt passion.

Before I knew it I was a student teacher for Kalamazoo Public Schools at Hillside Middle School. My mentor teacher, Mrs. Loftus, was excellent, and Principal Dorothy Young ran a tight ship. I discovered quickly that I was fairly ignorant in many teaching aspects but had a heart for students in urban middle schools.

I crossed the stage of WMU in 1994, with a bachelor's degree in Secondary Education. I decided to substitute teach in the area schools while awaiting a full-time teaching position. The adventures were endless. At the public high school I could be told to "F*** off" one day, and on another day could have kids leave the class for the bathroom only to be escorted back thirty minutes later by a security guard. On another day I'd be at a Christian school where the kids thought they were getting away with something because I let them go get a soda from the vending machine during class. However, unlike some of my challenging students in the public school, these kids would return promptly and get right back to work––no escort needed.

In the spring of 1995, I had two job offers on the table. One was at St. Joseph Public Schools (in the town I left before moving to Kalamazoo) and the other was at my alma mater, South Christian School in Kalamazoo. I opted for the latter. The first thing that I realized was that I had been promoted from the "Take-some-classes-college-party-fun-guy" to the "Christian-role-model-for-young-Einsteins."

In my first year of teaching I must have worked one hundred hours a week. While I did have to drag my butt out of bed every morning, I absolutely loved building relationships with the kids and getting them to enjoy math. When I began teaching the Bible to my eighth grade homeroom, I realized I needed to change some things in my personal life. I was a hypocrite. How could I teach these kids about faith or their walk with God when my walk was sketchy at best?

But, in my desperation and weakness, I actually began to grow in my relationship with Jesus. I began to seek Him. I began to hear and know the Holy Spirit. Instead of just someone who saved me from hell, Jesus started to become Friend, Brother and Lord of All.

Professional and spiritual development was strongly encouraged by the administrators. One part of that growth process was the chance to attend the Christian Educators Association convention in Milwaukee, Wisconsin. The CEA was always a great time. We would learn and be inspired at mass meetings and sectionals. We would fellowship with staff. We would dream. We would cast vision.

My colleague Joel and I attended a workshop called "Hallways of Grace" led by Pastor Bob from Indiana. Everything he said regarding the spiritual and social climate of our schools put a charge in us. For the first time in my life I was challenged to think about my personal mission statement. As I paused to reflect, something flashed like lightning in my spirit. The words came like an immediate spiritual download: *"To reconcile the body of Christ. To unite hearts who have been falsely separated. To really need each other."* It was so powerful that I wrote it in the cover of my Bible.

Within the next few minutes the room seemed to fade away. I seemed to be in an intense daydream that included seeing a building through some trees. I had no idea the type of building it was or where it was located. Then, I heard a voice clearly say, *"I want a Christian school in the inner city of Kalamazoo. And I want it to be affordable to anyone."*

Pastor Bob was still speaking as the room came back into focus. It was obvious that Joel and the others had no idea what I had just heard or saw. It had been about ten years since I last heard from God to become a teacher. Now I wondered if I just heard God again.

After returning to our hotel room I told Joel and Kevin, "I think God spoke to me." They nodded and smiled. They were used to me being a bit radical and passionate at times and may have been waiting for the punch line. To break the awkward silence Kevin asked, "So, where are we going for dinner?"

***

The years went by. I had been teaching at Kalamazoo Christian Middle School for nearly fifteen years now. The experience had been life changing. I had taught more than 1,000 beautiful, wonderful, amazing students during my career and was even presented with the Excellence in Education award after being nominated by a former student. At the same time I had become more intimate with God.

In my fourth year of teaching I married my beautiful colleague, Amy. We eventually had two children, and like my parents I wanted my children to have strong biblical names. For our first son, we decided on the name Isaac Matthew– the names together meaning, "Laughter is a gift from God." Our family grew with the birth of our daughter, Josiah Esther, which means, "Jehovah upholds the stars." We raised our children in the church and had a good life. But, something began to stir in me as I asked, *Lord, what do you want to do through me?*

It had been almost five years since God gave me the vision of a Christian school in the inner city. For the first couple of years I didn't even know what it meant. I often thought, *Hey, that's really neat that God told me, because when somebody builds that school I can say that God told me first.*

But things had been stirring in my soul. The pressure to start this "school" was growing every day and felt like an itch I couldn't scratch. So I started to get feisty with God. "What the heck do you want me to do about this? I don't know anything about starting a school, let alone one that will charge almost no tuition!" I had millions of questions but heard nothing from God.

One day during my devotion time I prayed about this school. I needed a word from the Lord, so I flipped open my Bible and landed on Joshua 18:2 which read, "How long will you wait to take possession of the land I have already given to you?" I knew on that day God was speaking to me about the school. He was beginning to line things up.

In 2004, we were led to move from our suburban home in the Parchment Township into the Edison neighborhood on Kalamazoo's south side. God had placed a burden on our hearts to raise our kids in a diverse community. We felt the diversity of the Edison community would provide an opportunity for our children to grow up around various cultures and ethnicities.

The Edison neighborhood was not one many flocked to. In fact, most were trying to get out. The one-hundred-year-old neighborhood contained residents with an average income of $22,000, which made it the city's largest population of poor. It also housed the city's most popular strip club. Many of the homes were large historic structures that just needed some love. Through all of its blemishes and shortcomings, Amy and I were led to a home on Lay Boulevard. It was up for sale, but the realtor said buyers were completing the paperwork to move in.

Our belief that God led us to that home was confirmed when the realtor called a few weeks later and said the other potential buyers' deal fell through. The house was ours if we still wanted it. We had already left our former church and joined The River church located on Portage Road right in the neighborhood. We would go through months of attempts to sell our own home, but in the end, we made our home on Lay Boulevard. We had moved to the area God had called us. We had found a church dedicated to love, serve and disciple those in our new neighborhood.

In January of 2010, the customary intention slips were put in our staff mailboxes at Kalamazoo Christian Middle School. Because our contracts were annual, the answer each teacher placed on the slip would let administrators know if they planned to return to teach the next year. I had grown to love every year at Kalamazoo Christian Middle School. But, for the first time in fifteen years, I checked the box that said, "I do not plan on returning next year." It was now my turn to step out and do what God had asked of me. Happy Birthday, Jesus!

CHAPTER 2

Out of My Shell

It had taken me seven years to be brave enough to step out in faith and not return to my secure job as a teacher. Did I have any more answers to my questions? Nope. But I had conviction and I needed to move. My dad taught me a great deal about being a person of integrity. I had purposely told very few people over the past five years about this vision to start a school in the inner city for low- income students. Why? Because I knew had I started telling a lot of people, I would have actually had to do something about it.

George Castanza of the TV series, *Seinfeld,* once proclaimed that every instinct he had was wrong. His friend, Jerry, brilliantly deduced that if every instinct he had was wrong, then the opposite of his instincts must be correct. Thus, using the wisdom of George, I deduced that if I had been disobedient for telling no one about this vision, then telling *everyone* would be obedient.

I went home, prayed, wrote and then sent the following letter to everyone I knew.

THE LORD HAS CALLED US TO START A NEW SCHOOL

Thursday, April 10, 2008

God Can Use Anyone

It's 7 a.m. The Lord woke me up at 5:30 a.m. this morning even though I'm on spring break. I showered, ate breakfast and have been praising God with the help of some Christian music on iTunes.

This day has been in the works for five years.

God gave me a vision to start a Christian school in the amazing Edison neighborhood where my family and I live. The people here are wonderful and diverse. It is a joy to walk amongst the 10,000 people here. Slowly but surely, God is shaping my heart to the level of love and passion He has for the people in this neighborhood.

Edison is the poorest neighborhood in Kalamazoo County. Poverty has many faces here—— financial, emotional, mental, spiritual, physical, support systems, role models, etc. Christ came so that ALL can have life to the fullest. So together we're going to form a school based on renewal and redemption. This is a school where ANY kid from this neighborhood can come and find Jesus in every aspect of life. There are no financial barriers. There is only hope, transformation and truth. In this school kids will learn about God, His people and His creation. They will be loved, cared for and supported. They will find their Purpose in life. They will learn how to make a difference in this world for Jesus.

I Need Your Help

I need a multitude of prayers for this venture. I know that some of you are already praying about this. If not, I would appreciate your commitment. Just e-mail, call, or write me back about how often you'd like to pray – every day, every other day, once a week, once a month or whatever. Just let me know when you plan to do it. If you know someone else who would be interested in this, please forward it to them. PLEASE, do not feel guilty if you don't want to! Only do it if the Spirit calls you!

Prayer Items

Praise God for He is Good! Praise for his patience with me. Praise God for his Spirit of reconciliation in this world!

Pray for the formation of the Vision Team. Pray for me that I will pray every day for this school. Pray for humility and obedience. Pray this school will start in the next 3 years. Let's reclaim this neighborhood for Jesus!

I Can't Stand Mass Mailings

But, they're a great way to get the word out. So if you're looking for something a little more personal about this vision, I will CALL you, WRITE you, or VISIT you.

Prayer is Not Enough

If it were, we would all be monks. I am in the process of discerning which individuals the Lord wants on the Vision Team. The purpose of the Vision Team will be to meet regularly to discern the vision, curriculum, staffing, and building needs for the school here in Kalamazoo. If you are

*sensing the Spirit is calling you to this, please contact me, and
the Vision Team will pray with you about it.*

In Christ,

Adam Sterenberg

The word was out. Many thought I was crazy––including me! But
there were a few who jumped in right away to pray and discern how they
might help build this school. Some of those who caught hold of the vision
were members of The River church. My family had joined the church in
2006 and enjoyed the powerful worship and teaching. The atmosphere
seemed to allow much more freedom in worship than I was used to. We
began to meet more people who had a heart and calling for the Edison
neighborhood.

The church held a conference entitled *Dunamis*, a Greek work for force
or power. The purpose of the conference was to help people understand
the Holy Spirit and His power. I needed to go in order to continue hearing
from God for answers and directions about this crazy school thing He
kept bringing up.

During the conference we did a lot of learning and praying––way
more than I was used to. At one point, we had to go to others and ask for
them to pray over us. I went up to a middle-aged couple and told them
about this vision for the school. They were both teachers! The gentleman
prayed that this chord of one would become a chord of two, then a chord
of three, which would not be easily broken. The woman prayed and told
me that she already saw a building for the school in place. Tears welled
in my eyes.

Then He sent Nate…

I met Nate at The River. He was the embodiment of the Rainbow
Coalition–– Black, White, Hispanic, a scholar, yuppie, hipster and thug.
You never know if he would be wearing ripped jeans and a T-shirt or a
suit. One moment you may catch him in the middle of a prank, and the
next minute he could be delivering a mind-blowing sermon. He had been
conducting street ministry on the south and east side neighborhoods of

Kalamazoo for more than ten years. Their goal was to meet the needs of people *as* they met them on the street. They would talk with people and hand out hot dogs and water bottles in the summertime and chili and hot cocoa in the winter.

They got to know people at grill-out events they hosted in the communities, oftentimes just outside liquor stores, gang houses or gas stations. They simply asked the people they encountered, "How can we pray for you?" It was simple. It was amazing. It was effective. It was like Jesus.

One day Nate came to The River and taught a class. I was deeply moved and convicted when he asked everyone who lived in the Edison neighborhood to open their homes for Bible studies. By doing that, he felt he would have plenty of places to refer the people he met along the streets interested in a Bible study close to where they lived. Amy and I looked at each other and knew instantly that this was one of the main reasons God had moved us into the neighborhood.

Amy and I seemed to know what the other was thinking even before anything was said. It had been that way ever since we first met in 1998. She had come to South Christian School to work part-time in Academic Support and part-time as a first/second grade teacher.

"You know, she's single," said my veteran colleague, Jim, who felt his 26-year-old friend needed a girlfriend.

"Thanks, I know," I replied.

After our first staff meeting I introduced myself to "the new girl," who had just moved to Kalamazoo from Grand Rapids. In my small talk I asked her where she lived. She said Walnut Trail apartments. Not wanting to seem like a stalker, I asked her what street, and she said 630 Charlie Court. This was scary; I had to ask one more question.

"What is your apartment number?"

"I live in apartment 2B."

"No way!" I said in amazement. "That's the EXACT apartment I just moved out of a few months ago!"

I think she was glad that I didn't live next door to her, but it didn't stop her from taking me up on a date to go rollerblading——no ulterior motives. But God had other plans. I liked everything about her. We laughed at the same things, liked the same foods, and she didn't mind riding on my motorcycle. After a month I asked her to "go steady."

After nearly a year of dating I took Amy on a ride to Battle Creek and took her to dinner at Clara's on the River restaurant. After dinner we walked along the river where I stopped, got down on one knee and began to ask her to marry me. Before I could even get the whole sentence out, she said, "Yes!"

Now I was asking her to take a ride with me on this vision God had placed in my heart. We agreed to hold the Bible studies in our home even after we had experienced some scary moments as new residents of the neighborhood. One night we came home after eating out, only to find human feces on our kitchen floor. It seemed some kids had come into our home right through our carelessly unlocked door.

In addition, after we gave yard work to a couple we felt we could bless with work in exchange for a small fee, they later broke into our home and stole my wife's inexpensive yet sentimental, family jewelry. Amy was crushed. What had I done? Across the street was a gang of boys who simply liked to play loud music and smoke drugs all day. One day we even saw a fully geared S.W.A.T. team lurking around our house, only to see the culprit they were searching for jump over our backyard fence. Could I put my family in danger by allowing strangers into our home?

We decided to trust God. Nate provided us with some powerful and relevant teachings to share with our attendees. I began to see Jesus in a whole new light. I was beginning a journey of learning what was most important in life, and what was not. By this time I felt I could trust Nate with my vision. After I told him, he was so excited and offered to do anything to help. Part of me wished he would have called me crazy, but he didn't. He would become my second of the three "cords" of strength that was prayed over me to build the school.

Then He sent Keith…

The River church contained another important player in the building of the school. I would have never guessed it would be Keith, who had dated a former high school classmate of mine. In our high school years Keith loved to sing. I didn't like him as was so dramatic and expressive when he sang. Our lives crossed paths again after college. We both married amazing Godly women. We wound up being youth group leaders together at Centerpoint church.

When we joined the River (a branch of Centerpoint) Keith was one of the pastors. He still liked to sing and dance expressively––only now it was to worship God. One day he danced so hard for God he blew out his knee. I liked Keith's passion for God and His people and was glad to worship and serve with him. I approached him with my vision. While he was excited for me, he also began telling me numerous things I should be doing. With each suggestion he made, I shrank further into a mental fetal position of doubt.

He then said, "I will do anything I can to help you get this vision off the ground." Suddenly I felt a huge weight being lifted. What a gift! I wondered if this was how Moses felt in Exodus 4:14 after God charged him to free his people from Egypt. Moses was afraid to approach Pharaoh on his own because he felt he could not speak well. It was then that his brother, Aaron, came towards him and was charged with speaking for Moses to Pharaoh.

It had been confirmed. My chord of two had become three. But even in my confirmation I was still perplexed. I didn't know where to start to build this school. I had more questions than answers.

We met at 6 a.m. one morning to pray about this school. I started begging the Lord to reveal all the details for His plan. The other two in my cord trio quickly smelled my lack of faith.

"Adam, I want you to take this in the nicest way possible, from one brother to another," Keith said carefully. "I'm just hearing from the Lord that you are being disobedient."

With that Nate snapped his fingers and pointed at Keith. "That's exactly what I was hearing!" he confirmed.

Because none of us had ever started a school before, we felt it best to put together a board of those who could help with the task. The board members would have various talents needed to help the vision become a reality. Because I was so anti-business and anti-formal, I didn't want to call it a board. I decided to call this group the Action Team, a.k.a., the A-Team. Unlike traditional boards, we didn't have people with money, influence or connections on our team. They didn't know how to start a school either, but they were devoted to the Lord and praying for the school.

Then He sent Jennifer, Stacie and Sonia...

Our friend, Jennifer, whom we met after moving into the neighborhood, was part of our house church. She quickly came on board the A-Team. Stacie, who worked for the neighborhood Big Brothers/Big Sisters organization, was in as well. And Nate's friend, a pastor of a Latino congregation, encouraged his wife, Sonia, to become a part of the team.

In July of 2008, we met for the first time at my house as the A-Team. I made barbeque chicken that was underdone. We prayed and talked. When we realized none of us had ever started a school, we did what those in the 21st Century do. We googled, "How to Start a Christian School." Our second listing on the search had an article of how to start a school in eighteen months. We read through it together. We agreed to set a start date for the school to open in the fall of 2010. Why not, right?

CHAPTER 3

The Trifold

We came at this vision from the top down. The first thing we needed was a name for the school. We threw around such names as *One, Solid Rock* and even *Promised Land*. I don't remember when it happened, but I was led to the name, *Tree of Life*. It resonated powerfully in my spirit and was mentioned in three places in Genesis, Proverbs and Revelation.

Now we needed a powerful logo that would represent us well. Because Nate was the artist of the group, he was charged with coming up with something that would be used on brochures, T-shirts, everything associated with the school. When he came by with his first draft, I was blown away! It had the tree with the cityscape and the fruit of the Spirit hidden in the leaves. He had a guy in the trunk of the tree holding a kid, but to me, that looked kind of creepy. I asked him if instead of the creepy man, he could draw the lines in the trunk to look like a hand reaching down from above pulling up a hand from below. He came back with his second rendition. It was perfect.

The next thing we worked on was a vision statement. The mission and philosophy statement followed close behind.

Tree of Life Vision

Renewing young minds. Transforming young lives.

Tree of Life Mission

Tree of Life exists to provide a Christ-centered education to all children regardless of their socio-economic situation. Tree of Life celebrates the diversity of the body of Christ and equips children to serve God, people, and creation to their fullest potential.

Tree of Life Philosophy

Tree of Life is a distinctively Christ-centered school located in the Edison neighborhood. This is Kalamazoo's most populated, economically challenged and diverse neighborhood.

Our main purpose is to provide a transformative biblical education to a broad range of children who may not normally have the opportunity to do so. The Bible will be applied to all areas of life.

Students will learn to think creatively, worship enthusiastically, analyze critically, live wisely, and love unconditionally so that they may transform the world around them for the glory of Almighty God.

And with a few more pieces of information and some pictures, the Tree of Life trifold brochure was born. We printed 500 full-color copies. To us, we were official. We now had the first and only tangible element of the school. We had something to hand out to everyone we knew and those unsuspecting parents who we felt may be interested in a quality, Christian school in their own community.

We flew through those brochures in no time. The thought of the cost of full-color brochures was too much on our already limited resources. Instead of full color we just started printing them in black and white using Astrobright Terra Green paper. By default, that became our school color.

As the seed of Tree of Life began to sprout, The River was outgrowing its building on Lake Street. A larger facility was offered to them in a prime location downtown for a $1.99! I was on the Elder team that prayed together about whether to move out into the new facility away from the neighborhood, or stay in a building that wouldn't allow potential size growth. The team was split right down the middle and discussions were oftentimes heated. Eventually we discerned both sides were right. God was calling us to split so we could multiply. The River eventually moved downtown across from Bronson Park. Keith and Nate were called to plant the new church named Vanguard.

Through an amazing set of God stories, the leadership discerned that Vanguard was to be located in the factory building on Fulford Street. I couldn't believe it when they mentioned the location. It was the very building that Amy and I walked past when we first started taking walking tours of our new neighborhood. The two-story factory was built in 1869. I remember distinctly walking by it and feeling a strong pull towards the building. I remember saying to Amy, "That would be a cool place for a Christian school." At that time the building was not for sale.

The River would now take over the building. They gathered its troops and more than $100,000 to renovate the 10,000-square-foot building. As they worked, Amy and I prayed on whether we should leave The River and join Vanguard. Our decision to move was confirmed during a fishing trip with a brother in Christ. I told him I didn't want to be known as a "church shopper" but felt drawn to move. He then told me many reasons why this was a perfect fit for our family. His final words were, "It's almost as if this church has been made for you." I knew he was right.

Vanguard opened its doors in 2009. I could feel the love of God the minute I walked through the door. The Holy Spirit was potent. The worship was powerful and intense. The teaching was convicting and inspirational. The prayer was profuse and earnest. The Body was diverse with Black, White, and Hispanic; young, old, rich, poor, gay and straight—just like our neighborhood.

In the summer of 2009, as Vanguard established itself in the community, the A-Team began working to get our word out. We made a concerted effort to go door to door to announce the Tree of Life School to the 10,000 residents of the Edison neighborhood. Because there were just a handful of us, Keith suggested we solicit help of the Vanguard house churches located in the neighborhood. We gave each house church a section of the neighborhood to blanket with our brochures.

We felt we needed one big event to draw attention to us and decided to throw a block party. With the help of my friend, Eric, we chose Reed Street Park, right in the heart of the neighborhood. We provided food, fun and fellowship to the nearly 300 people curious enough to see what we were about. It was crazy to think that we spent about $1,000 to tell the neighborhood about a school that didn't yet exist in the natural. About twenty-five parents filled out interest forms, which was a *huge* encouragement for us.

The block party wasn't the only place we would show our bright green brochure and vision. Our volunteers manned a table at such neighborhood events as National Night Out, Hispanic American Council parties and the popular WOTV television's annual Miranda's Park Party. We wanted to do anything and everything we could to get the word out.

Then He sent John…

While our effort to begin a school from scratch seemed an overwhelming undertaking, God brought a man into my life as a witness that it could be done. Just fifty miles away in Grand Rapids, Michigan, The Potter's House was established in 1981. This urban Christ-centered school also began with twelve students using space in a church basement. As we worked to hand out our brochures to get kids to attend, The Potter's House was serving 550 students in grades Pre-K through 12th on two campuses. Like our vision, the school celebrated its diversity and affordability to anyone.

Then He sent Wayne…

What better mentor than someone from the Potter's House to keep me encouraged. I soon reached out to John Booy, one of the founders and superintendent of the school. His stories and advice were an immense encouragement topped off with his powerful prayers for our success. In addition to John, a man named Wayne who was a supporter and friend of the Potter's House was a great resource. He was a successful businessman in the business of connecting people. We had lunch together, and I shared some of my own struggles and doubts about Tree of Life. He shared notes he had taken from a speech that inspired him.

*How do we know it is a vision of God
as opposed to a bright idea?
(These thoughts come from notes on a speech by Robert Lupton)*

- *Chaff of bright ideas blow with the wind.*
- *Kernel of vision takes on a life of its own.*
- *Don't have to worry about forgetting it; it will not go away.*
- *It is authored of God.*
- *Not out of human intelligence.*
- *Coincidences will start converging around it that make you know you are not in control.*
- *Can't take credit for it.*
- *Has magnetic capacity that draws people from all directions and places.*
- *Always bigger than your capacity to deliver.*
- *Brings people of God together for a redemptive purpose.*
- *Its essence is faith.*
- *Has a certain germination period that makes its timing difficult to predict.*
- *Danger in premature launching.*
- *Not much danger in going slowly.*
- *Has an appointed time; Spirit of God ignites it.*
- *Like a balloon, you can't tell its shape, color, etc. ahead of time; don't know its final outcome; it moves with the Spirit.*
- *Energizes people but takes a lot of energy to get started.*
- *Authored of God, conceived in the mind of God and entrusted to people.*
- *Role of visionary is to be the primary guardian of the vision; maintain the integrity of the Vision and protect it from well-intentioned people; provide support and protect the integrity, but not to grasp or control it.*
- *Visionary is primary storyteller, not the owner of the vision.*
- *Visionary is probably not the manager of the vision.*
- *Born of faith and carried by faith; the wind of the spirit will take it where it needs to go.*
- *Vision energizes you; gives you life.*
- *May have a premature death (God adjusting the ownership).*
- *Timing involves daily sensitivity to the leadership of the Spirit.*
- *Vision casting is different than vision receiving.*
- *God's work done God's way will never lack for God's supply.*

CHAPTER 4

Do You Trust Me?

The momentum for Tree of Life was increasing. There were many signs and wonders. There was no turning back. It was time to give Jesus His birthday present. Doubting God at this point would have been detrimental to the vision.

Before the close of the school year and my venture towards the vision, one particular day started off as a normal teaching day at Kalamazoo Christian Middle School. I woke up at my usual 5:30 a.m. to spend time with God before going to teach my students. But this morning was like no other. I planned to let the principal know that after fifteen years I would not be returning to teach in the fall.

I went downstairs to our family room. For some reason I didn't turn on the lights. I just sat on the couch in the dark. I really didn't have much to say to God. He knew why my heart was pounding. I was about to do the craziest thing of my life. In my mind I emphatically said to God, *You know why I am here.*

Some time went by and then God spoke to my heart.

"Do you trust Me that I will bring you the teachers you need?" Right away with confidence I said, "Yes."

"Do you trust Me that I will bring the students you need and the students that need you?" A couple of minutes passed. I said, "Yes."

"Do you trust Me that I will provide for you and your family?" Time passed. I don't know how long I sat there. Eventually, quietly, confidently, I said, "Yes."

Then there was a fourth question. "Do you understand that I have it all?" I wept, fully realizing I had a peace that passed all understanding.

Through a great deal of conversations with God, it became evident that He wanted me to be the principal. In April of 2010, the A-Team decided it was time to hire teachers. We had no building, a couple thousand dollars and about seven committed students. But, we felt we had to move forward in preparation. With the help of Dave, who was president of Christian Schools International, we posted a job description on their website. Our first job-posting read:

> *Tree of Life is a Christ-centered urban start-up in Kalamazoo, MI. We will open this fall serving grades K-3. We are looking for two Michigan certified teachers (¿se habla español?) to serve the youth of Edison neighborhood - one K/1st and one 2nd/3rd teacher. If you are called to teach young children, are passionate about justice, and willing to die to yourself, please contact Adam Sterenberg at treeoflife.ateam@gmail.com or download applications at www.tolschool.org*

We were praying, but I was constantly thinking, *who on earth is going to respond to this?* After a month seven people had sent in applications. I called each person for unscripted phone interviews. I wanted to be led by the spirit to discern if they were a fit and to let them know the reality of what they would be walking into.

Then He sent Pam...

One evening I called Pam. She was my least favorite teacher on paper because she had so many past jobs on her resume. I started off by asking her how she was doing.

"Well, I'm a bit sore," she said unenthusiastically. I thought, *Sheesh, how old is she?* She then elaborated.

"Well, I was playing rugby with the kids at recess, and one of them clipped me pretty good."

She was tough. She got involved with the kids. I was starting to like her. As the conversation progressed, I was taken in by her story. She described herself as an Ojibwa Canadian Mennonite. She had been teaching for two years at a school in Big Grassy River First Nation, which was two hours from Winnipeg, Manitoba. Her husband lived in Grand Rapids so she commuted thirty-two hours round trip every six weeks to visit him on weekends.

I let her know that we *hoped* to pay her $25,000 a year, without benefits. At the time we had practically nothing in the Tree of Life budget, and the parents' tuition would not cover our salaries. She said that was okay and believed that the Lord would provide. I thought, *Okay. She's crazy too.*

The A-Team invited her to Kalamazoo for an interview. She came dressed in a very nice business suit. I rode my bicycle to the interview and was dressed in shorts and a T-shirt. Other members of the team dressed nicely—Nate wore athletic pants and a jersey.

After asking basic interview questions, we allowed Pam to share her story with us. We learned she had been homeless as a child before being adopted by her aunt and uncle. They enrolled her in a Christian school; however, she had rejected the Lord. After graduating high school she traveled overseas with a friend and had even gone to Russia. By age 20 she had a son, was a backup singer for a Heavy Metal band and could take apart and rebuild motors. She was tough. While working at a group home, she had been stabbed by a patient. Another time a 300-pound patient knocked her down and sat on her chest for three hours before someone came to rescue her!

Pam confessed that only four years ago she began her relationship with God. That experience was the result of her stumbling upon a church in Minneapolis late one night, desperate and lost. She said she went to the front of the church, knelt down, threw her hands up in the air and said, "I give up. I need you!" She had been following Jesus ever since.

While hearing her stories our eyes and mouths opened wider and wider. The A-Team did not discuss long. It was unanimous. Pam was to be the first teacher.

Then He sent Jessica…

Jessica was attending college on the east side of the state in 2007 when she received a vision from God about starting a Christian school in the inner city. Although she was really excited about starting a school someday, she didn't have a lot of direction. Upon her graduation she told the Lord she would go anywhere in the world to teach––anywhere but Michigan, that is.

A week later she stumbled upon our online job posting. Although she felt convicted to apply, she didn't because it was in Michigan. After several sleepless nights God told her that she would be unable to fall asleep until she applied for the job. She obeyed.

Jessica's application looked very good. She was new to the field of education; however, she had a lot of experiences that would be very beneficial. During her phone interview I learned that the well-traveled 23-year-old had been to twenty-six countries, owned her own photography business and coached gymnastics. She had grown up in a home without Jesus but gave her life to Christ at the age of 15, after her parents divorced.

I set up a Skype interview with the A-team and Jessica because she was teaching Bible school at an orphanage in India on a short-term mission project. The interview went well. We now had Jessica, and another candidate to choose from. We knew Pam was in but were split on the decision of the other teacher.

During 5 a.m. prayer at Vanguard, I pictured myself in the Father's arms. I repeated, "*I just wanna hear your heartbeat.*" It was very peaceful. I was enjoying His presence. I wasn't thinking about anything, just listening to His heartbeat. Suddenly I heard Him say one word, "*Jessica.*" I was surprised, but I knew exactly what that meant. I later shared this with the board. We unanimously decided to hire Jessica. She was so excited to hear the news, and we were thrilled to have her a part of the school family.

A year later I found out that Jessica said she *knew* she was supposed to be at Tree of Life but sensed she wouldn't get the job. She told God, "I know this is where I am supposed to be. You have to tell them they are supposed to hire me."

To that I said, "Thank you, Jesus!"

CHAPTER 5

Location, Location, Location

Then He sent Father Mike…

For a long time, we thought Tree of Life would be located on the upper level of Vanguard church. While we had an architect sketch some rough plans, I did not sense that it was supposed to be there. When John had prayed over me, he prayed that God would give us a space where we could incubate. We began to look at renting space somewhere in the neighborhood. Keith had suggested looking into St. Joseph Catholic Church on Lake Street. The church had operated a K-12 school in the neighborhood for almost one hundred years before they closed five years prior to our search. We wondered if they would be willing to rent space to us.

I contacted Father Mike of St. Joseph. I learned very quickly that he was an amazing Spirit-led man of God. I pitched the idea of us having a Christ-centered school in the upstairs of their former school building. He liked the idea and his council approved. Thank You, Jesus!

In August of 2010, one month before the first day of school, we signed a two-year lease. I thought it was never going to happen. We used two of their large classrooms. There was one for our combined K-2nd graders and the other with our 3rd-5th graders. A gym, playground and janitorial services were included in our contract.

We began to share our desires, passions and needs with everyone we could. We let people know we trusted the Lord for the $100,000 needed to pay for salaries, rent, curriculum and classroom needs. We really had no idea where all the money would come from, but we trusted Him. To the glory to God, we had about $20,000 in donations by the first day of school. Vanguard had allowed us to organize under their ministry as our fiduciary so our donors could provide tax-deductible donations.

Donations of classroom supplies and books began to roll in. We kept my front porch unlocked at all times as a drop-off point. There was so much school stuff on our porch that I lost my tennis shoes in the bounty. I had remembered taking them off on the rocking chair that was now under a mountain of stuff, and I had to perform acrobatics to reach them.

Pam and Jessica came by and sorted through the items. 85% of what was donated was taken to the classrooms, and I could see my porch again. Two days later it was full of donations again. I was in awe of how the Lord loved these kids. Once the teachers got their classrooms set up it looked as if they had been teaching there for years. We had everything we needed and so much more. Glory to God!

I felt an urge to get more word out about Tree of Life through advertising. It needed to be something that would be very effective in our neighborhood where there was no shortage of "pimped-out" (decorated) cars. I got this crazy notion to paint my 1999 Saturn a super bright yellow green to match our trifold. In spite of estimates that it would cost nearly $2,000, I found one guy who said he could do it for $400, but his shop was out of business.

Vanguard decided to give Tree of Life a $500 seed for our ministry. I decided to use that money to paint my car. One of my former students at Kalamazoo Christian Middle School told me that his dad, Jeff, painted cars. I called Jeff and asked iif he could paint the car, hubcaps and all, for $500. I had already bought a quart of finish coat for $175. He agreed. When Jeff pulled the finished product from behind the barn, we all said, "Whoa!" and burst out in laughter. The paint job looked professional, but it was so stinking bright! Jeff admitted that painting the hubcaps was a nice touch.

My next plan was to get a door magnet put on the side of the car. My dad suggested I should talk to a guy named Paul who did car graphics. Paul emailed me back with three mock-ups of my '99 Saturn, all decked out in graphics. I kindly let Paul know that we really already went over in budget on the paint job and had little left for extravagant design. He insisted I select the one I liked the most.

A few days later I went to his shop. He wanted to have his designer, Trevor, teach me how to weed the decals, put them onto transfer tape and prep the surface of the car. All along I was praying, *Dear Jesus, I sure hope he's not going to make me put these on the car!* But Paul completed the work without me, and it looked phenomenal. When it was complete I asked him how much I owed for the work. He started crunching numbers and said, "$40." I was blown away. Jesus in action again!

Every day the car did its job. As I drove around in the giant yellow green billboard I saw at least one person a day with their mouth saying, "Tree of Life School." I even spoke with a cashier at a store one day about the school and she said, "Oh. Is that the green car?"

***

Two days before our first ever Tree of Life open house Amy came to me while I was in the shower. She relayed the message that the fire marshal wanted me to call him back. My heart nearly stopped. We had made two assumptions at this point. First, we were a small Christian start-up school receiving no state funding and didn't need to register with the Michigan Department of Education. And second, the space we were renting would be grandfathered by the State because it was a school just five years prior. We quickly learned we were wrong on both accounts.

I was beside myself. Over the next forty-eight hours I cried out to God, consulted the A-Team, researched and called lawyers. I was constantly on the verge of throwing up. *How could God bring us this far and then bring it all crashing down?*

According to the state, we were about to start an illegal school in a non-compliant school building. We could be fined, jailed or shut down. We tried to look for every loophole without being deceptive. I asked the A-Team if we should continue or pull the plug? They said to proceed until someone from the State shut us down. That was easy for them to say, they were not the ones who would go to jail. I would!

Ken, the regional fire marshal, told me that in order to be "grandfathered," it had to have been an operating school within the last three years. Otherwise, the building would be considered new construction. We would then have to meet EVERY current building code and could not occupy until all codes were met. That would cost hundreds of thousands of dollars and take several months to complete assuming St. Joe's was agreeable to it.

I tried to call Tony, the top state fire marshal in Lansing. I explained to his secretary that I desperately needed to talk to him to give us a temporary permit until we could get something figured out. He was in Detroit at the time; however, his secretary relayed my message, but my request was denied. I called her back the next morning and offered to buy her flowers, donuts, anything she wanted if I could just talk to her boss.

While driving to a meeting at Panera Bread restaurant, I was crying. I was holding my phone and muttering, "Come on, call me, just call me. JUST CALL ME!" And then the phone rang. My heart skipped a beat. It was Tony. I poured my heart out to him and explained that we were just a small Christian school trying to reach out and help underserved kids. I continued my plea by telling him that we would only have twenty students and the building was totally safe with a modern fire alarm system. I told him we weren't getting any state funding because we were not even registered with the Michigan Department of Education.

"You're not registered with MDE?" he said confused.

With tears in my eyes I said, "No. Do you want us to be?"

"Let me call you back in a minute."

He hung up leaving me with little hope. In my despair I got to Panera and sat down for my meeting. Inside I was a mess. Our open house was that evening, and I couldn't concentrate on the person who was talking to me. Then the phone rang. It was Tony. I hustled outside to take the call in private.

"If you're not registered with the MDE, then we have no business with you. You're off our radar," Tony said.

"Are you kidding me?"

"Nope," he assured me. I began to laugh.

"Well, you just made my year, Tony! God bless you!" I danced a jig praising God right there in the Panera parking lot.

TOL Quick Facts 2010

- 12 Students in grades PreK-3.
- 75% of students are minorities
- One principal, two teachers, many volunteers
- $100,000 annual budget. 90% met by donations. 10% met by parent's tuition.
- Renting two classrooms at St. Joseph's Catholic Church.
- 50% of TOL families have a single mom as head of the household
- 75% of TOL families are on some form of government assistance
- 50% live or have lived in the Edison Neighborhood
- 50% of TOL kids have little or no church connection
- $18,000 average income for TOL families

CHAPTER 6

The Twelve Little Disciples

A few weeks before school opened, the *Kalamazoo Gazette* ran an article about our school. A couple of days later, a man named Jerry called me saying he was the superintendent of Heritage Christian Academy located in the suburbs of Kalamazoo. He had read the article and was thrilled with what we were doing. He and his staff had been praying for us.

"I know that you're reaching a group of kids that we'll never reach here at our school," Jerry said. "We'd like to do anything we can to help you."

I thanked him for his call and for the prayers. It seemed almost too good to be true. Christian schools didn't partner, did they? Was he a used car salesman? I really wasn't too sure what to make of it.

The week before school started, I was talking to Amy about how the Lord had provided everything, the teachers, books, supplies, money, a building and even a volunteer art teacher. God had provided everything except a music teacher, and the kids really needed one.

A day later, Jerry called. He reassured me that he and his staff were praying for us and asked, "Do you need a music teacher?" He said their music teacher, Marilyn, had a block of free time on Wednesday mornings that she could use for professional development or observing other schools. She had suggested using that time at Tree of Life. I was speechless. Eventually I told him about my conversation with my wife, Amy, about that very subject. We now had a music teacher.

Jerry really wanted to find more ways to partner. He would bring our staff coffee, donuts or bagels. He invited us to his staff in-services and paid for our staff to attend their professional development conference. He always called when they were getting rid of things that we could use and had even invited our students to be part of their school Christmas program.

Our first half-day of school was September 6, 2010. It was surreal. We prayed for forty kids and 12 kids showed up. There were nine kids in Pam's PreK-1st grade classroom and three in Jessica's 2nd – 3rd grade classroom. I said a silent prayer, *Oh, Lord, there are only twelve kids. Who's going to support a $100,000 ministry for twelve kids in an illegal building?* He responded in a still small voice, *"I don't care about the numbers."*

I moved past the unimportant. There were twelve children and they were *beautiful*. They were diverse and from every walk of life, every culture, social stratus and level of relationship with Jesus. They were here to learn about God and his creation. They were here to reach their full potential in Christ. It was utterly amazing. Even though the world was screaming about how many things had been done wrong, my spirit knew it was *right*. My Papa was proud, and the enemy hated us even more. This had been such a battle. I realized that God was fulfilling His second promise. He had sent the students that needed us and the students whom we needed.

A Seedling - A New Creation
September 8, 2010

Glory to God! We are celebrating God's goodness in starting Tree of Life! Praise God for the 12 students that have become part of the TOL family! They are amazingly beautiful group and it is a joy to serve them. They are already learning so much about the amazing love of Christ and the world that he has created!

Parents have been overjoyed to have their students showered with Christ's love. Whether parents know Jesus or not, they can see the difference in a Christ-centered education.

Pamela and Jessica, our super-dedicated teaching staff, have been working countless hours to prepare the classrooms and lesson plans. Their faith and devotion to Christ and these children is amazing!

Our theme verse this year is "'Love the Lord your God with all your heart and with all your soul and with all your mind and with all your strength.' The second is this: 'Love your neighbor as yourself.' There is no commandment greater than these."

On the first day, I invited parents to stay for morning worship. There were permanent risers in Jessica's classroom so we had the kids sit there. I got up front with my guitar and started to play worship songs geared towards children. Most of them just stared. I was sure that many did not know what to make of it, but I pressed on and worshipped the King.

At the end, I introduced our school verse of the year from Mark 12:30-31: *"Love the Lord your God withal your heart, soul, mind and strength, and love your neighbor as yourself."* I also explained that we would have a new verse each week, and those who memorized it would get a quarter. That got them excited.

All the students discovered TOL in different ways. Some of the students came by open house, some via flyers in the neighborhood, news articles in the paper and word of mouth. The first to come—our twelve little disciples—were Judah, Sasha, Isabelle, Kiera, Kaytra, Patrick, Harmony, Isabell, Isaac, Angela, Nivea and Princess.

Isaac

We knew we were going to have at least one student at Tree of Life––my amazing son, Isaac. In fact, that was the only guarantee we had early on. Amy would stay at home with our younger daughter, Josi, while I worked as principal for Tree of Life. Our income was just $3,000 above the poverty line, which led to us qualifying for some government insurance for the kids and food stamps. Through it all, we considered it a joy and an honor to follow Jesus into this great endeavor called Tree of Life.

Isaac had attended a Christian school in the past; however, we felt very convicted that he needed to be part of his neighborhood Christian school and its diversity. He adjusted well and, as a second grader, loved school and taking care of the classroom tortoise, Reggie.

Sasha

Sasha's mom, Sonya, was the editor for a free magazine publication called *Community Voices*. It was a West Michigan publication that focused on positive multicultural news. Sonya came to interview me at school a few weeks before we started to profile us on her website. I was always eager to share what God was doing and told her one miraculous story after another about how God used us to bring the school into existence.

By the end of the interview, Sonya asked if she could enroll her daughter. I was so excited to offer her a place in the TOL family. Later, her husband Sean became a member of our board. He owned his own graphic design company and helped create our website and marketing materials.

Sasha was a beautiful and vibrant little girl who did her best for Jesus while in kindergarten. As the youngest of four kids (her oldest brother was a musician in New York City) she came to Tree of Life and immediately made lots of friends.

Siblings: Harmony, Isabell (Izzy) and Patrick

About two weeks before school started, I was driving down by Upjohn Park on the south side of Kalamazoo near our neighborhood. I wanted to turn left onto Walter Street but noticed there was no left-turn sign. I had to drive the long way around the park. Frustrated and in the heat of the day I noticed a row of houses we had missed with our flyers. I parked the car and ran a trifold to each house. As I reached the last house, a mom pulled up in a van full of kids. They piled out as I walked up to the mom who had a lit cigarette dangling from her mouth. She seemed pretty stressed; however, I took it upon myself to tell her about our school. She told me that her kids were always getting into fights and chasing boys at school. She said she would love to send them somewhere different and immediately—on the roof of my car—she filled out an application for her three children. I was overjoyed!

Harmony was assigned to Jessica's third grade class. She had a beautiful smile and a compassionate heart and was often making cards thanking me for Tree of Life. She was the oldest of seven kids and took it upon herself to water the plants in her class and read the Bible during her free time.

Her mother attended the local community college while struggling with anxiety and bipolar disorder. Harmony's father died a week before school began. Harmony was known as a bad kid at her old school where she chased boys and fought girls. Her mother said she would often have to call the school principal to urge Harmony to get out of bed and go to school. At Tree of Life Harmony had become a leader and was excited about coming to school each day.

Isabell had so much love inside of her. She loved to play the Djembe during our worship time every morning. She, like her sister, Harmony, also was known as a bad kid at her old school. She was about a grade behind academically, and we felt she had Attention Deficit Disorder. In the beginning of the year she and her siblings came to school with cereal and cookies for lunch. Thanks to teachers, volunteers, and the local food pantry she received a healthy lunch. Later, she and her siblings would attend church with our family.

Patrick may have only been in kindergarten, but he was the only kid who could go all the way across the monkey bars on his own. While small in size, he was strong and loved to run and play outside. Since coming to Tree of Life he had learned a great deal of how to treat others with respect and love. Patrick was several years behind in some areas and often stuttered, but had overcome so much.

Kaytra

We had met Kaytra and her mom, Nichole, three times. We first met her while canvassing the neighborhood with our flyers during the neighborhood National Night Out event. We met her again at the first Tree of Life block party. Every time we talked, Nichole was super excited about the school and really wanted her daughter to attend.

A couple of days before school began, I was driving around the neighborhood near Kaytra's house. Her family was sitting on the porch grilling. Technically, Kaytra was a few weeks too young for kindergarten, but we were flexible.

Once school started, I often picked up Kaytra in our yellow-green official school car. She was always polite and constantly telling her mother that she loved her. She lived with her mom and sister. Over the past two years she had lost her grandma and great-grandma who lived in Kalamazoo. This left them without any family support. Without transportation it was hard for her mother to get work. Without funds, stable housing also was a challenge.

Angela (On-hey-la)

Angela and her parents, Tim and Mia, came to the open house a few days before we opened. When they received a Tree of Life flier in their mailbox, they could not believe it. They prayed their daughter could attend a good Christian school they could afford. They signed her up right there and then.

Angela was a bright and beautiful young girl. She seemed shy; however, she was a little spitfire. Her mother is Hispanic, so her ability to speak Spanish during our lessons on basic Spanish made her a class leader. Her dad moved to Texas where he worked to send money home. He called the school a week before it opened, excited to talk to me about Tree of Life.

Judah

Judah's mom, Monifa, was the first mom to ever fill out an application. She met us at National Night Out one year before we opened. She said she was trying to turn her life around and wanted something different for her son.

A few months before school began I tried to contact her. A man answered the phone and began to chew me out. He called me a punk and said he knew what I was up to. After he finished his rant, I kindly told him that I was the principal of Tree of Life. He got pretty quiet and then told me he'd have her call.

I didn't hear back from her by phone but received an e-mail from her. She apologized for not getting back right away and asked for prayers concerning a recent news report of abuse to her by a former boyfriend.

By the grace of God, Judah made it to Tree of Life and was such an amazing addition to our school. The kindergartener wore some of the sweetest braids in his hair that I'd ever seen and a great big smile to go with it. He lived with his mom, grandparents, older siblings, aunts and uncles who helped take care of him while his mother worked swing shifts at group homes. His mother told me that she wanted to make changes in her life, and she wanted her son to be part of a Christian school because she knew it would make a difference in his life as well.

Isabelle (Belle)

Belle lived three doors down from our family. I shared with her parents our goal to open Tree of Life school. They had been looking for an alternative to the neighborhood public schools; however, the other area Christian schools were way out of their price range. Her dad was manager at a local restaurant, and her mom started her own dog grooming business. Both parents were graduates of Michigan State University and loved to go to Kalamazoo Kings baseball games.

I could tell they were a bit apprehensive, but before long, they enrolled Belle. Every day during worship she requested we sing "Jesus Loves Me" and attempted to sing louder than anyone. She worked hard on her alphabet and numbers.

Kiera

Kiera was the daughter of one of my former students. Her grandma used to give me rides to school when we had only one car. She heard about Tree of Life through her husband who saw me handing out Tree of Life flyers at an event. She told me about Kiera and the many struggles she faced at home. Kiera's dad was diagnosed with mental illness, was rarely around and had no income. Her mother was a full-time student at Kalamazoo Valley Community College who worked as a nanny on weekends and could not possibly afford any other Christian school. We were a Godsend for Kiera.

Kiera would come to school every morning with a bright smile. The kindergartner loved giving me "fives" that were so hard they made my hands hurt. She sang the loudest during morning worship on songs. Her work ethic was great as she worked hard on learning her numbers and alphabet.

Princess

Princess's mom, Rosa, found out about us through various neighborhood events. In addition, our school was in the building next door to where she worked as a receptionist, a building also owned by St. Joseph church. She really wanted Princess to be at a Christian school as she said her daughter had picked up a lot of bad habits at the public preschool she previously attended. I assured her that income wasn't a barrier, and she was thrilled to enroll her daughter.

Princess was a beautiful girl who, much like her fellow kindergartners, worked very hard on her numbers, alphabet and days of the week. She could be shy at times, but because she was bilingual, she often shined the most when it was time to learn Spanish. Princess and her mom lived in an apartment and attended church on Sundays.

Nivea

When Nivea was little, her mother was in a serious car accident that caused brain trauma. Although still highly functional, the 22-year-old mother had the mental capacity of a 15 year old. She was living on a huge insurance settlement that was to supply her needs for the rest of her life. An organization was assigned to oversee her finances and care.

41

Nivea's Aunt Judy heard about us and wanted something different for her niece, so she enrolled her in Tree of Life. During school I would often overhear Nivea singing praise and worship songs in the bathroom at the top of her lungs. The kindergartener also developed in her education and made new friends. In the meantime, she was suffering from abuse. Her Aunt Judy found out that the family caregivers were stealing the trust money and beating both mother and daughter. One day, Nivea told Judy, "I don't want to get hit anymore." Aunt Judy, Mom and Nivea began coming to church and all were baptized. Praise God!

All of the students, each with their own special personalities, challenges and contributions, had become the first class of Tree of Life. Just one month after school began the kids had gotten into their routines and learned all the worship songs. Each morning they would sing their hearts out for the Lord before starting their daily lessons. They would dance, close their eyes and raise their hands. If we missed worship for one day for some reason, they would get upset. In the meantime, the word about Tree of Life continued to spread even after school began. Two more students were added to our family.

Lydia

Lydia was friends with Harmony who enrolled at Tree of Life with her siblings. Lydia's mom heard about all the good things happening to Harmony's family as a result of being a student at our school and decided to enroll Lydia. We were excited to have her join us in November.

Isabel (Inez)

At the end of October, Darcie called me and talked to me about bringing her kindergartner, Inez, to Tree of Life. She was dissatisfied with her current school for a variety of reasons that included bullying. We were all set to receive

Inez the next day. I told Pam and her class that a new student named Inez was coming. They were so excited! This would mean one third of our students had the name, Isabel, which means, "dedicated to God."

The next day came and went but Inez never showed. Her mom was sick but assured us Inez would be in school the next day. Her anxious classmates kept asking about her. I told them that they should pray for Inez. Needless to say, days turned into weeks and weeks turned into months. I knew the family was struggling with health issues, but Inez never came. Yet every day the unprompted kindergartners prayed for Inez to come today. Even though the kids kept praying, I know we adults had long since given up.

On January 16, 2011, I received a voicemail from Darcie. She apologized for not getting back sooner, but she was still 100% sure that she wanted Inez at Tree of Life. My excitement was reserved at best. The next day Inez and Darcie showed up! Glory to God for the kindergartner's great faith!

PART 2

Sapling

*"Stay here in this land. If you do, I will build you up
and not tear you down; I will plant you and not uproot you."
Jeremiah 42:10*

CHAPTER 7

Miraculous Provision

On the third day of school, the Michigan Department of Education left a message on my cell phone––otherwise known as our school phone. It said I had to register our school with the State of Michigan, and they would send a copy of the law stating that fact.

Again, I hit an emotional bottom. I was thrown right back into the darkest pit. If we registered, that would trigger a fire and building code inspection. If that happened, we would surely be shut down. I prayed and prayed. I wish I could say that I didn't worry, but I did. We tried to think of every loophole to get around this gigantic hurdle; however, none of us on the A-Team could.

In the meantime, as kids continued to show up for school, sing their hearts out for Jesus and excel in their academics, we kept the issue super quiet. Only a handful of people even knew about it. I didn't want the teachers to be concerned, so I only asked them to pray that God would spare us from any issues from the State.

One morning I went to 5 a.m. prayer at Vanguard church. I was pacing around, praying and crying. *What a mess, Lord! Help us, Lord!* Then I heard him whisper, "Don't worry, you're gonna keep your classrooms." I felt a wave of relief hoping that I had really heard God.

We analyzed all our options with the State and came to another profound conclusion...don't call them back. Days stretched into weeks and weeks into months. They never called us back. *Thank you, Jesus!* We were not trying to beat the system. We wanted to play by the rules of the State as long as it didn't compromise our mission. So we needed to find a state-approved school building in the neighborhood, and fast.

I was pretty sure that we could not start a second year knowing that our building was non-compliant. We pressed into the Lord. As we pressed on, God brought others on our team to help in ways we desperately needed.

Then He sent Dad…

Shortly after our school year began I talked with my dad. I knew that my passion for keeping financial records was weak. Thankfully, God had given Dad an anal-retentive spirit, which works out great for bookkeeping. I handed him an envelope stuffed with receipts and checks. I was so relieved when he said that he would volunteer as our treasurer.

He set up things on QuickBooks and learned all that he could. It was a huge learning curve for both of us. There were many tense moments. But because of my dad, we had bank accounts that balanced and financial records that could stand up to any audit. He worked tirelessly, passionately and for free. His relationship with the living God grew by leaps and bounds and so did our relationship. Bless the Lord!

Then He sent Roger…

During our early days at The River church we met a nice couple, Roger and Heidi. The few times we connected it was apparent that we were kindred spirits. When they heard about our school opening, they asked me to lunch. I told them all about what God was doing and how he was transforming and renewing the kids and our families.

I mentioned that our staff was going to visit Potter's House School in Grand Rapids for professional development. Roger suddenly blurted out, "Can I come?" I thought for a minute and said, "Sure." I was quite baffled by this, as was Roger.

During the visit in October our teachers went along to observe classrooms. Roger and I talked with Nate, the development director. We started talking about our need for a state-compliant school building and plans to renovate Vanguard church— an upgrade that could be as much as $500,000. Nate started throwing out strategies. At the same time he began to ask Roger what role he played in all of this. Before we knew it, Nate started giving some sort of altar call to Roger.

"Roger, is it possible that in your third trimester of life that God is calling you to give your all to something extraordinary?" I really wasn't sure what was even happening. I don't think Roger did either. We were both mystified by what God was doing.

About a week later, Roger asked me to go to his house for lunch and prayer. As we talked, he made it clear that he had a role to play at our school. He expressed how his heart just melted every time he saw a picture of the students. I said he needed to become a member of the A-Team. He said that he just needed a title. He quickly became our Development Director.

His intentions were to do things in the traditional sense, but God turned it all upside down. Instead of spending most of his time fundraising he spent more time with facility acquirement. He may not have realized it then, but the greatest thing he did was to help develop me as a Spirit-led CEO for Tree of Life. He helped hold up my arms when I was weak.

Then He sent George...

People asked me all the time, "Where does all the money come from?" I would say, the Lord. They would ask about what big donors were on our board or what churches were supporting us. But there weren't any. I would tell them again that we were blessed in miraculous ways from the Lord. I would say, "If you can explain it another way, I'm open to it."

We didn't do a lot of fundraising; I never liked the thought of it. I used to call it the "F" word until Keith gave me a book by Henri Nouwen called *The Spirituality of Fundraising.* In the book Nouwen claimed that you should ask people everywhere at all times for financial help in Kingdom work. He had excellent biblical arguments that helped redeem the concept of fundraising for me, but I still did very little to actively *ask* people for money.

In fact, the harder I tried, less came in. As time crept along I did less asking and more praying. But I was happy to share stories of what God was doing through regular communications that included praises, requests, testimonies and needs. We mailed these newsletters to about 250 people three times a year. We sent monthly communications to the nearly 350 people on our mailing list. Sean, Sasha's father, was one of our board members. He used his graphic design skills to help us develop a beautiful and effective website where people could donate through PayPal. We even created a Facebook page.

I was still learning how to lead a school and craved any information that would help. I remembered that John, from Potter's House, suggested I read Arthur Pierson's book, *George Mueller of Bristol*. Bristol was a great disciple of Christ who started orphanages and Christian schools in the mid-to-late 1800s in England. As I read about his life in Christ, he quickly became my new hero. When he began his first orphanage, he wrote:

> *The three chief reasons for establishing an Orphan House are:*
>
> *1. That God may be glorified. He should be pleased to furnish me with the means, in its being seen that it is not a vain thing to trust in Him; and that thus the faith of His children may be strengthened.*
>
> *2. The spiritual welfare of fatherless and motherless children.*
>
> *3. Their temporal welfare.*

Mueller's approach was to let no one know the need. He would only pray to the Lord and ask for things. That way, only the Lord could get the glory. I knew that God was calling me to be more like that.

One of the verses that quickly became a mantra for me was Matthew 6:33: *Seek the Kingdom of God above all else, and live righteously, and he will give you everything you need.* Another was 1 John 5:14-15: *And we are confident that he hears us whenever we ask for anything that pleases him. And since we know He hears us when we make our requests, we also know that He will give us what we ask for.*

It took me nearly two years to read this book as every five pages or so blew my mind. Each day I read it seemed to coincide *exactly* with what was happening at Tree of Life. My faith in the Lord continued to grow.

My dad called me one night with news about our school bank account. He said we needed $1,300 to make payroll for that next day. I said, "Ok. I don't know what you want me to do about it. The Lord knows our need and He'll provide." I wasn't entirely confident.

We had staff devotions the next morning, and I decided against mentioning the possible lack in funds to pay the teachers. As we began to dismiss and prepare for students, Pamela remembered something. "Hey, I almost forgot," she said. "My mom called me last night and said her church took an offering for Tree of Life, and they are going to send us a check. It should be here any day now. She said it was like $ 1,300."

I almost cried. It was then that I shared with them the conversation I had with my dad the night before. Those types of things continued to happen to allow us to pay every bill on time. Some paychecks were a little late, but we never missed one. We never lacked anything, even the many times God came through at the last minute. I had grown up hearing that's how He works; otherwise what we ask and believe is without faith. More and more I understand this truth.

Even though my unanswered prayers of providing just four donors who could contribute $10,000 each, it was evident God wanted to show His power. About halfway through the first school year my prayer changed to, *God, I hope we don't get any big donors so that you'll just be using a bunch of regular people to make this thing work.*

And that's exactly what He did. Our average donation for the first year was $400. Our largest donation was $3,500. We didn't have any big backers, and we didn't have any aces in the hole. But we had God. He proved to be more than enough.

The parents' tuition only covered about 10% of our annual budget. The remaining 90% came through donations from individuals, churches and businesses. About 15% of our donors have made regular commitments to our $100,000 first-year budget projections. We started with $20,000 in hand.

As things moved along by faith, I remembered a note a friend wrote me when we were struggling with funds to open. The note said that we should seriously consider pulling the plug if that was all the money we had. It was an arrow to the heart. I didn't blame him. He was just being practical. But my spirit welled up as I told him that we were no longer walking by sight, but by faith. It may have sounded pious, but I had never felt weaker saying it.

People constantly asked where the other $80,000 was going to come from. I had no idea. I was terrified. But the manna always came. That's what Dad liked to call it. With manna there is never too much, just enough.

I often had a student who would come up to me and stick some loose change in my hand. I would ask what it was for, and he said it's for the school. The prayers of students and staff would oftentimes be answered by those who had no idea what we were praying for.

After we moved into the school, donations once left on my porch were now placed in the hallway outside our classrooms. Sometimes I knew about a donation coming; sometimes I was surprised. Not only was God providing for the kids and staff, but those families as well.

One day, I walked upstairs to our classrooms to find a complete bed set stacked in the hallway. My first thought was, *"Ugh, now what I am gonna do with that?"* Immediately, the Lord brought Inez's mom, Darcie, to mind. I called and asked her if she needed a bed. Her response was that of sheer excitement. Her kids were without a bed and had been sleeping on the floor.

Darcie had a life story filled with depression, pain and abuse. But, when she became part of the Tree of Life family, she began to experience hope. One day she called me very distraught. The previous day some youth drove past their apartment and fired more than thirty rounds into the downstairs apartment. Most of the bullets went into the apartment below; however, five of those bullets came through the walls of her upstairs apartment. By the grace of God, absolutely no one was hurt.

She shared how one bullet came through the wall where someone was typically sleeping on the floor. Even more so, her elderly friend who lived in the apartment below used oxygen tanks. There were two tanks sitting right in the front room and neither was hit! The Tree of Life family sprang into action with prayer and love.

Our next challenge was to figure out how to get this complete bed set to her house. She didn't have a car, and the Tree of Life car was too small to transport the bed the nearly two blocks from the school to her house. A few days later, a volunteer group of eighth graders from Kalamazoo

Christian Middle School came over to volunteer their time and play with our students. Then it hit me.

During lunch, I had each volunteer grab part of the bed. We marched down the stairs and down Lake Street carrying parts of the bed. It was quite a sight, and, of course, people were staring. We got to Darcie's and marched it into her upstairs apartment. She was so grateful and the students were glad to be a part of it. I think that was the first time many of them realized how they took even the smallest comforts for granted. Many had never experienced true need or poverty. Darcie wrote a huge thank you to the donor who had prayed that the recipient of the bed would be blessed and know Jesus. The donor later befriended Darcie and blessed the family with meals, gifts and friendship.

I've often told people it's a miracle every day at Tree of Life. Whether it's someone drawing closer to Christ, moving up a reading level, scoring a run in gym, or financial provision, it's always a miracle.

The first few months of school in 2010 were financially tight. We didn't spend money on anything unless we really needed it. Jessica really insisted on being ecofriendly. Therefore, the original twelve kids ate their lunch on IKEA plastic ware. I felt it was my daily duty to do all the dishes. The best place to clean the dishes happened to be the janitor's closet because the bathroom sinks were too small. The janitor's closet was about four feet by five feet wide. It had a deep mop sink that was about two feet off the ground. It would get a little crazy in there sometimes because the hose on the end of the faucet would get away from me. My back would often be sore from bending over for a half hour. I soon realized this was an act of love, an act of worship.

One day, the teachers told me we had run out of paper plates. I also needed more dish soap. Our first round of supplies had been donated. I went to the Family Dollar right around the corner and felt slightly ill to my stomach. I prayed, *Can we afford to buy this stuff? Is it okay?* I found my two items and went to the cashier. My total was $2.12. I remember telling the cashier that we were tax exempt. She said she didn't know how to do that. I finally resigned to letting her run it with tax. I thought, *I hope this doesn't break us.*

In addition to us believing that we were to be good stewards of the funds God had provided, we also believed that He had created our bodies to be temples of the Holy Spirit. We were to care for our temples, and we encouraged healthy eating habits. During lunch, Jessica would often have her students eat a fruit or vegetable. She would provide it to them if they didn't bring their own.

Fruit and vegetables were often considered exotic or toxic foods to some of our kids. Making them eat one shortcut carrot for lunch was like giving a veritable death sentence. There was a great deal of groaning, crying, excuses and dry heaving.

Harmony was especially "allergic" to naturally grown foods. She walked up to me one morning with a crumpled piece of paper from her mom that read: "Please do not make Harmony eat any more fruits or vegetables." I kept that note. It made me laugh and cry and the same time.

A Seedling - Lemonade Stand
July 26th, 2011

When children are led by the spirit, amazing things can happen. That is not more evident than in this story about Connor and Kaden.

One day, the boys asked their mom if they could do a lemonade stand. Mom said sure and asked what they wanted the money for. They shrugged their shoulders. They said they didn't want anything. Mom asked if they wanted to give the money away. They agreed that would be a good idea. When asked whom they'd like to give it to they said, "How about that new Christian school we talked about?"

They made large colorful signs and a big tree where people who donated could write their name on a leaf and then post it on the tree. They set up their stand at their father's job. They had a ton of people come through to their stand and were so excited to tell people about Tree of Life School. When they finished their sale, they came to see the school and presented me with the tree naming all the donors plus a coffee tin loaded with $132!

I always tell people that every penny counts. In fact, if it wasn't for the lemonade stand, we would not have been able to pay our staff that week. Thank you, Jesus, for so many families following your lead!

CHAPTER 8

Baptisms

Harmony
January 2011 by Jessica

Last Wednesday in class I asked the kids to write in their prayer journals. I asked them to write what they knew about Jesus and what else they wanted to know about Him. They had about ten minutes to think and write down what they knew including any questions they had. Afterwards we had a discussion about who Jesus was and what they already knew. Halfway through our discussion Harmony proclaimed, "I'm ready to make the decision today!" I clarified with her that she wanted to make the decision to invite Christ into her life as her Lord and Savior. She excitedly confirmed.

I asked her if she wanted us to stop our discussion and pray and make the decision right there and then with her friends. She decided she wanted to wait till later when just she and I could talk and pray together about it. A few months prior to this I had shared the salvation story with the students. At that time Harmony said that she wasn't ready to make the decision to give her life to Christ and needed more time to think about it.

A few weeks before Christmas break I felt the Spirit of God nudging me, telling me to share the message of salvation with her specifically again. I explained to her that God had asked me to share the message with her. I challenged her to think about why God was asking me to share this with her again and if he was calling her to act on what she had learned about his saving love and grace.

Later in the day Harmony and I met one-on-one to talk about the decision to invite Christ into her life. I asked her to explain to me what this meant to her and how her life would be different after she made this decision. It was amazing the depth of understanding she had about what it was Christ had done for her and how he desires to have a personal relationship with her! She told me that she had spent a lot of time over Christmas break thinking about this and that she knew she was finally ready. We prayed together, and with great joy she invited Christ into her life to be her savior and friend forever!

It was so beautiful to see her come to this decision and to spend so much time thinking about it. She has had a lot of anger and bitterness towards God for different things that have happened recently in her family. Slowly he has been softening her heart and melting away her anger, turning it into a sincere love for him. The next day during Writing Workshop she wrote a beautiful sincere prayer thanking Jesus for what he had done for her and how thankful she was that he was in her life now.

Izzy
March 2011 by Jessica

57

Wednesday afternoon in class we were discussing the verse for the week, "If you confess with your mouth that Jesus is Lord and believe in your heart that God raised him from the dead, you will be saved." As we were discussing the verse Isabell excitedly proclaimed, "I do believe it, I really do!"

We talked about how Jesus died for us on the cross and died to save us from our sin, so we don't have to suffer being separated from God because of our sin. The kids learned that we needed to be saved from ourselves, and our sins, daily, because we can't do it on our own. We need Jesus to help us and do it for us.

During this time of discussion I shared my testimony of how I made a decision to follow Jesus, declaring that He was Lord of my life and that I would live for Him. I explained how when we invite Jesus into our lives to be our forever friend. We choose to follow Him and the way that He calls us to live.

I explained the enormity of what this decision meant and how it doesn't make your life perfect or mean that everything will be easy. But it means that you will have Jesus with you always, and He is the only one who will never disappoint you, never stop loving you and never leave you.

After explaining to them that they too could make the decision and commitment today to follow Jesus with their life and make Him their friend forever, I gave them some time to think and pray about it. A few minutes later, Isabell excitedly came over to me and said, "Well, I did it! I made Jesus my forever friend! He's going to be with me always!"

I explained to her that this was the best decision she could ever make in her whole entire life. We spent a few minutes praying together. Closing in prayer with a genuine heart full of gratitude she said, "Thank you, God, for letting Jesus die on the cross for my sin. Thank you for saving me, and thank you for being my friend forever."

Kamren
October 2013 by Jessica

Yesterday during our Bible study time in the morning the third-fifth graders were learning about Jesus's great love for us, and what he did for us on the cross. *We talked about what it meant to accept His gift of eternal life and how He gave himself up as a sacrifice for us.*

The kids took time reflecting on where they were with their relationship with God and had time to make a decision to invite Christ into their life if they never had before. Kamren had never invited God to be a part of his life and decided that today was the day. He asked if we could pray together and if I could help him make the decision to invite Jesus into his life. Praise God that there is one more kid in his kingdom!

Patrick & Darcie
April 2011

We rejoice with the angels as both Patrick and Darcie (Inez's mom) were baptized on Resurrection Sunday!

Pat was with his mentor, Jason, at The River when he decided he wanted to be baptized. He and Jason went up front to talk with the elders who confirmed Pat understood what baptism meant. He then proceeded to show the church that he had asked Jesus into his heart and wanted to live for Jesus.

Darcie was with her daughter, Inez, at Vanguard church. There were five candidates to be baptized; however, Pastor Mike discerned there were more being called. We praise God for Darcie being one of seven more who came to receive Christ and declare Him as Lord of their lives that day. I give her credit too, as she agreed to be dunked in the cold water without an extra set of dry clothing to change into.

"God made us alive with Christ. God raised us up with Christ, and seated us with him in the heavenly realms," Ephesians 2:5-6.

Tarra
2013 by Nate Bull

We went to Vanguard church to celebrate as a family on Easter. My mother-in-law came as part of that group. She had been struggling in her walk with the Lord and didn't want to get baptized until she was sure about her commitment.

The Easter service was wonderful. There were several scheduled baptisms— and some spontaneous ones. Although the call was extended to anyone else who felt led to be baptized that day, my mother-in-law wasn't one of those people. I don't think we even asked her; it didn't occur to us that she would do something like that.

After service we went home with one of the Tree of Life students we invited to share lunch with us. As lunch was being prepared, the conversation turned to the service and the baptisms. The little girl from Tree of Life, who didn't have family to eat with that day, began sharing her testimony of how she gave her life to Jesus by getting baptized.

My mother-in-law was convicted and went into my bathroom with her sister and my wife. After an hour of talking and worshipping, they came out to announce that my mother-in-law wanted to get baptized in our bathtub! We filled it up and dunked her down.

It was a glorious experience.

CHAPTER 9

Mountain Ranges

Then He sent Brent...

Since we needed a state-certified school building, we really started investigating space at the Fulford building, home of Vanguard church. For a time, I really thought that Tree of Life was going to relocate above Vanguard's sanctuary. I shared our prayer request with Pam and Jessica. Pam mentioned that her husband, Brent, was a structural engineer who would be happy to come and review the potential space.

The two visited Vanguard one Sunday and went to check out the upstairs after service. We took measurements and discussed possible layouts for class space. Brent later sent preliminary drawings but suggested we talk it over further with an architect.

Then He sent Robert...

Brent's boss referred us to an architect named Robert. I called him one snowy November, and we talked as I supervised the kids on the playground during recess. I told him a bit about our school and he immediately said, "I get what you're doing. I will do whatever I can to help you."

What a huge blessing! I told him about agreement to rent space above Vanguard if we paid for all modifications to the building. Robert then started spouting off all the codes that building needed to meet in order to be a school. The first was that kindergartners and first graders aren't to be housed on the second floor. He went on to list other issues such as certain percentages of natural light with respect to wall space, sprinkler system, etc. My head was spinning. Who knew there could be so many codes?

Robert came from Grand Rapids to Kalamazoo to review the space that Amy and I envisioned years ago would be home to our school. After careful consideration, he broke the news to me slowly.

"I'm not going to tell you that you can't build in here, but you need to consider a few things," he said matter-of-factly. "First, you're not going to own the building, so you'll be paying rent. Second, you're going to sink more than $200,000 into making this space work for just two or three classrooms. Third, you're going to have high utility bills in this old factory building. You'd almost be better getting a chunk of land and building something new."

"Well, there isn't a lot of vacant land laying around in our neighborhood that would be suitable for a school."

He then looked out the windows and said, "What about all this land right out here?"

"It's not for sale. I know it isn't. The lady who owns it is leasing the sidewalk and parking lot to Vanguard. She's letting us use the parking lot on Sundays only." I left it at that.

Every day that passed from the start of Tree of Life I saw His mighty hand in my life. I saw it in the teachers' lives. I saw it in the kids' lives. I saw it in the parents' lives. I saw the seed growing into a sapling. I became more confident that the state was not going to "uproot" us.

One day Father Mike of St. Joseph Church, who leased the space for the school to us, emailed me. He wondered if everything was sorted out with the fire marshal. I decided to tell him the whole truth and realized this could be grounds to terminate our lease agreement. We set up a meeting where I told him all the gory details. When I finished, Father Mike said, "We have a saying around here. 'We don't like to make Jesus look stupid.'" I laughed!

He said he would talk to his lawyer and see if there was any problem. He never called me back. Even though I was relieved we could keep our classrooms, my concern for the future grew intense. *God, don't you know that you don't build a school in a day?*

We began looking for other facilities to renovate, keeping Vanguard as a Plan B. We began to seriously consider a school building for sale that was outside of the Edison neighborhood. As I prayed about it one morning, I opened my Bible to the passage from Jeremiah 42:10-16:

> *Stay here in this land. If you do, I will build you up and not tear you down; I will plant you and not uproot you. For I am sorry about all the punishment I have had to bring upon you. Do not fear the king of Babylon anymore, says the Lord. For I am with you and will save you and rescue you from his power. I will be merciful to you by making him kind, so he will let you stay here in your land.*
>
> *But if you refuse to obey the Lord your God, and if you say, 'We will not stay here; instead, we will go to Egypt where we will be free from war, the call to arms, and hunger,' then hear the Lord's message to the remnant of Judah. This is what the Lord of Heaven's Armies, the God of Israel, says: If you are determined to go to Egypt and live there, the very war and famine you fear will catch up to you, and you will die there. That is the fate awaiting every one of you who insists on going to live in Egypt. Yes, you will die from war, famine, and disease. None of you will escape the disaster I will bring upon you there.*

I knew that this Word was for me, and Tree of Life. If we didn't stay in Edison, the school would die.

Christmas came and went. I heard nothing specific from the Lord about what we were supposed to do for a school building. Then one day I stopped in Vanguard's parking lot to pray. I demanded angrily to God, "WHAT DO YOU WANT ME TO DO LORD? SHOW ME!"

A minute of silence passed. Then I heard a whisper. "I want you to get some land and build a school."

I laughed out loud. "That's *rich*, Lord! Really *rich*! We were a fledgling nonprofit Christian school with twelve kids. We're just hoping to make next week's paycheck, and you want us to go get land and build a school? Well, You're going to have to move a mountain, Lord! No. You have to move a mountain *range*. No. That's not enough. Make it *35 mountain ranges!*"

I shared what I heard with the A-Team and the staff. Rather than sit unmoving in unbelief, we plodded ahead. We were confident of what He said but unsure of everything else.

In February, Roger and I put together three building proposals to present to the A-Team. The costs ranged anywhere from $80,000 to $500,000.The first was to renovate and rent space in the Vanguard church on Fulford Street. The second was to purchase a lot next to Vanguard and set up some portables. The third was to purchase the lot and build a new school. I was so nervous.

We presented all the options, both pros and cons. We took a leap of faith and recommended proposal three. I was overjoyed, stunned and humbled when they unanimously approved our recommendation.

Then He sent Mike and Bill...

There was a land lot for sale on the corner near Vanguard. The owners were asking $40,000 for it, but soon after our meeting with Robert the asking price dropped to $20,000. Roger investigated and discovered it was little over an acre which is pretty big in Edison. The lot followed the curve of Bryant Street, which used to follow the curve of the train track to the industrial section. It was essentially a lot shaped like a 100-foot-wide banana. We thought maybe it would be possible to put a school there. But, we had no money.

Roger contacted the owners, Mike and Bill. Roger told Mike about our school and what we were trying to build. Mike told Roger, "We're very benevolent people." That got us excited.

Roger and I went to meet with Mike and had some great conversation. We asked Mike if we could have the land for $500. They gave us the land for free in exchange for a tax write off! When we walked out of

Mike's office, Roger stopped, threw his fist in the air, and shouted, "Yyyyyyyyyyyyyyes!!!"

Then He sent Gary…

We now had land. Now we needed a professional's idea about our sketches for a school built on the banana-shaped lot. Roger set up a meeting with Gary at a local design firm. When we met, Gary described what we could do on the piece of land we had been given.

"I'm not saying you can't build a school on this property, but it would be weird. You'd have a long hot dog-shaped school," he said.

He asked about the big lot–shaped like a shark tooth–that butts up against the big banana shaped lot. I shook my head and said again, "I *know* it's not for sale!" Then Gary said, "These are two of the craziest shaped lots I've ever seen. What if we just drew a north/south line right down the middle of the lots?"

Wow. That made sense. He suggested we then trade the top half of the banana for the tip of the shark tooth. Then we would each have a lot that was better suited for our needs. Whoa! We had never thought of that. It sounded brilliant enough to work.

Then He sent Karen…

Sean's graphic design office was located across the hall from the owner of the shark-toothed lot. Karen had watched his children grow up and had heard Sasha talk about her Tree of Life school. Sean set up our situation, and Roger and I made an appointment to talk with her. We told her about the school and showed her a picture of the kids so she knew who was being blessed.

When we asked if she would be willing to sell her land, she shook her head and firmly said she needed it for truck turn around and for future parking if she ever sold the warehouse that is near that lot. We then threw out Gary's idea. She looked at it carefully and said," Hmm. I might be able to do that. Let me go walk the property and I'll call you in a few days."

She called back a few days later and said she would trade the land for no charge! We now had a piece of property where we could actually build a four classroom school. God had moved mountain range Number One. I started to think maybe He wasn't kidding about this.

We were so excited about what God was doing in and through people. I asked Robert to be our architect. I told him that we really had no money, and he said, "I'm going to give you prices so low you'll think you're getting a huge discount."

He then proceeded to ask me about the rest of the design team. I said that Brent would be our structural engineer. He said he might know an electrical engineer in Kalamazoo. I said I would look for a mechanical engineer and sight planner.

CHAPTER 10

Preparing a Place for Us

When I was growing up I remember everyone in my family getting lice—except me. I always thought it was something you got when you were dirty. I believed it was a plague or something, and knew that once it was in the house you had to wash everything and throw things out and wash like crazy.

Since being a school principal I had become an expert on lice. When the first case was discovered in our classes I was again terrified. I thought, *are we dirty? Cursed? Had God's favor left us? Did we have to send everyone home and shut down the school? What are we supposed to do, Lord?*

Lice love people who have thick, dark, straight hair. They do not like hair that is oily, thin or loaded with hair care products. The adult lice looked like tiny brown grains of rice and crawl onto your hair or body from someone or something else. Since they are asexual they lay eggs like crazy and the eggs (nits) are like a tiny bead of glue on a strand of hair. They only come off if they are pulled off. To rid a head of lice, you need to inspect every single hair daily for a month.

One day Pamela reported live adult lice in a student's hair. We sent her home and had some experienced parents check the other kids. They found several students with nits. We called parents to come pick up their children. One of our new moms came in totally irate. She started accusing the teacher and the children of negligence. She went on about how her children never had lice. She collected her children, stormed out and the children never came back.

We didn't have a head lice policy, or barely any policies. I called my old school and learned they needed a student to be nit free for three days before they could come back to school. That seemed a little extreme, and when we tried it, we realized that with that rule some of our students would never be able to come to school. I called the neighborhood public schools and learned they only sent a student home if they had live ones in their hair. We adopted that policy and were extremely careful that children didn't share hats and coats.

However, there were always a few families who constantly struggled. I would buy special shampoo and nit combs. My wife and other parents would graciously go to their homes to help with delousing. I learned that's where the phrase, "nit picking" came from. It was an incredibly tedious job. We quickly understood why single moms with several children had a difficult time getting rid of them.

Then He sent Bruce...

Keith told me that Bruce was an engineer who helped them a lot with renovating the Vanguard space. I met with Bruce to talk about some of our preliminary plans. He began to alert me to all the approvals that we would need from the city. He also informed me about the Baseline Environmental Assessment (BEA) that would need to be done before we even officially purchased the property. That didn't sound cheap.

He said Phase 1 would run about $5,000. I thought, *Ugh. How many phases are there?* He let me know that we would probably need a Phase 2 and that could cost anywhere from another $5,000 to $25,000. "Give me some good news, Bruce." He gave me the names of some companies to call.

A few months later I officially asked Bruce to be the site designer. He was excited. We walked the property a couple of weeks later, and he discovered several old iron pipes that were painted blue. They ran right through the middle of our property. I told him I wasn't sure what they were. He said, "You better hope they're not markers for a high pressure gas line."

Again I felt mild panic, as that could be a deal breaker for the whole school. I checked with gas companies and learned it was not a gas line but easement for a fiber optic line. Praise God for another mountain range moved!

Then He sent Lance…

I got to know Lance a little bit at Centerpoint church. I really got to know him when he and his family came to Vanguard. They just showed up one day because God had called them there.

Lance later told me that in a quiet time with the Lord, God said to him, *"Go to Vanguard."* He said the command wasn't, "go check it out." He said it was more like, *"GO there now and don't look back."* He was a bit thrown. He talked to one of his best friends, Mike, who said he had heard the exact same thing! Lance lived about fifteen miles northwest of town on a micro farm. Mike lived about ten miles south in the suburbs. Vanguard was focused on the neighborhood, and they were clearly outside of it. Admittedly, they knew they were being called completely out of their comfort zone. Praise God they were both obedient. I quickly connected with them, knowing what it was like to be called out of your comfort zone.

Lance called one day and asked me to view a house that was located right behind my home. He wanted to buy it and rent it out to some folks at church who were looking for affordable housing. The house was dirt cheap and move-in-ready. After looking, Lance asked me to show him around the neighborhood. He was completely overcome by the stories and visible signs of poverty. His heart was being broken by what he saw. His spirit was heavy.

When we got back to my house, I shared with him what God was doing at our school. He ate it up. As we sat there, I felt a strong urge come over me and blurted out, "You need to think about being on our board." I had never felt that compelled before to ask someone something and realized later that was the Spirit's presence in a powerful way. Lance had moist eyes and quietly responded, "Yeah." A few weeks later he joined the board.

After Lance had been on the board for a month, I felt another strong urge. I called him one day and asked him to be our board president. He replied, "I'm really not qualified; I have no experience being a board president. I have more questions than I do answers."

I told him that's exactly who we needed as a board president. God worked with him over the next month, and he finally said he'd be willing to do it. After making a recommendation to the board, they unanimously supported Lance as president.

Then He sent Tom…

I called the first environmental firm Bruce mentioned to inquire about a BEA. I left a message with Dave and told him a little bit about what we were trying to do. When he called me back, I asked him a bunch of questions. He estimated Phase 1 would cost about $5,000. Phase 1 was primarily research about what kinds of companies existed on the land. Because we were in an old industrial zone, it would most likely require a Phase 2. That's where they would take soil samples and analyze them for hazardous chemicals. That would cost up to $30,000. I was not encouraged by the sounds of that.

I asked him how their business's prices compared to others in the area. He told me that they would most likely be higher since they serve mostly high-end clientele. I appreciated his honesty. Dave suggested a guy who could do the job for far less than he would charge. He gave me his number. *Did that just happen? Thank you, Jesus, for favor!*

I gave Tom a call. He grew very excited about the project and wanted to help in any way that he could. Roger and I went to meet with him and he felt he could do Phase 1 and 2 for us for $10,000. It was an amazingly generous offer, but still far more money than we had. We accepted Tom's offer in faith. We knew that he was our guy.

We experienced firsthand God's poor math skills and Tom's obedience to the Spirit. Every time I talked to Tom, the amount of work increased and our bill decreased. Tom encouraged me greatly and was a huge blessing, giving us a fancy 250-page legal document for a total of $2,600. We had just enough money to pay the bill. Glory to God!

Then He sent Josh…

I first got to know Kristin back when she was in youth group. She later taught at Kalamazoo Christian Elementary School. She and Josh were starting a family, and she wanted to be at home more. She had coffee with me one day and told me how she really wanted to volunteer. We were so blessed that she came in once a week as a literacy aid.

When we went public in March with the announcement of our building campaign, she told me that Josh was a mechanical engineer and would probably be able to help out with the design. He agreed to do the job as a volunteer. Glory to God!

Then He sent Greg…

Robert connected me with his friend Greg who was an electrical engineer. He was a super funny guy who loved what we were doing. He agreed to create the electrical blueprints for the building. He didn't charge us anything. I was again shocked and awed. Thank you, Jesus!

CHAPTER 11

The TOL Dinner

As spring of 2011 approached we felt a need to raise awareness and money for the building project. We felt led to have a dinner in May that would be a time to fellowship and celebrate the Lord, the children and cast the vision for the new school building.

We planned to have the dinner at Vanguard, feeling it important to have it in the building next to where the school would be. So many people helped spruce up Vanguard for the event. The plan called for twelve tables that would hold ninety-six people. Fancy linens and place settings adorned the tables, which were topped off with amazing mini cupcake centerpieces. Pastor "Papa" Mike and his house church catered amazing rib tips with all the fixings. Jessica and Elisha added ambiance to the place with floor lamps and white Christmas lights.

On the night of the banquet nearly every seat was filled. We decided not to charge but provide people the opportunity to give as they were led after seeing what God had done with our school. We showed a powerful video made by Drew and his crew, and the students arrived to lead worship for fifteen minutes. Jessica gave a powerful speech about how so many had been powerfully transformed. I closed with the following memorized speech written from the depths of my heart. The following is the exact speech in its entirety.

Family and Friends,

We are gathered here tonight for one reason— For the Glory of God. Truly, without Him and his unfailing love, we would not be here tonight.

For some, you may not know the beginnings.

About seven years ago, I was at a Christian Educator's Convention in Milwaukee. The sectional I attended was "Hallways of Grace". At one point in the session, the room faded away. I saw some things and heard God say, "I want a Christian school in the inner city of Kalamazoo, and I want it to be affordable to anyone." I later shared with a few friends what I thought I heard God say to me. I don't know if they thought I was crazy. I didn't know if I was crazy.

Glory to God!

A year later, my family and I moved into the Edison neighborhood. It was VERY different from what I grew up in. 10,000 people, very diverse, rich, poor, red, yellow, black, white, highest crime rate in the county. We were scared. But it sure increased our propensity to pray. And each day in many different ways, God replaced our fear with love. Our children were learning to live and play with a wide variety of people.

Glory to God!

For five years I was unwilling to receive the vision. I argued with God. I came up with more excuses than Moses. I told Him He was crazy. But our God is so loving and so patient! He listened. He waited. He consoled me when I cried. He encouraged me. And slowly, surely, he led me down the path. And then he disciplined me.

Glory to God!

Over two years ago, I told a couple of praying friends about this vision. They were immediately on board and offered help in any way to get this vision off the ground.

One day we met to pray about this vision. They both told me they heard from God that I was being disobedient. And, like our precious Father, he knew this was the kick in the pants I needed to get things going. So I went home and sent a letter to everyone I knew, telling about the vision.

Glory to God!

And the floodgates opened. People. Prayers. And even a little bit of unsolicited money. Wow. Was this real? Could this be happening? A board of six came. We started to meet once a month. How in the world do you start a school in this neighborhood——a Christian school affordable to anyone? Where's the money coming from?

Glory to God!

And then the Life began to grow. The Tree of Life is mentioned three times in the Bible——the beginning, middle, and end. And on each side of the river stood a tree of life bearing fruit and its leaves will be for the healing of the nations. A vision statement came – Renewing young minds and transforming young lives. And then a mission statement – providing a Christ-centered education to all children regardless of their socio-economic status, embracing diversity, and helping each child reach their full potential in Christ. How can we make it affordable to anyone? We'll charge 5% of family income regardless of how many kids they have. And the more people got involved, the more the vision became reality.

Glory to God!

In October of 2009, it became very real to me. One morning, I went down to spend time with Jesus. I didn't turn on the lights – I just sat in the dark and said to Him, "You know why I'm here." And, of course, He did. He knew that I was about to do the craziest thing I've ever done for Him. I was about to hand in a notice to Kalamazoo Christian Middle School with the box marked, "I'm not planning on returning next year." I was about to give up fifteen-years worth of relationships with people whom I loved and served dearly. I was about to give up the security of my paycheck and benefits and half of what I was making for my family of four.

I sat in silence for a while and He asked me three questions: [SLOWLY]

"Do you trust me that I will bring the two teachers you need?"... Yes

"Do you trust me that I will bring the students you need and the students that need you?"......Yes

"Do you trust me that I will provide for you and your family?" ....Yes.

"Do you understand that I have it all?"

Glory to God!

In the late spring of 2010 he brought two amazing teachers to TOL! In September, He brought us twelve amazing students! And as of today, Jehovah Jireh has supplied us with $80,000 from over 300 amazing individuals, churches, and businesses!

Glory to God!

The story may seem a little too focused on me right now. Let me be clear. It's not about me.

I could tell you more about the Godsend that Mrs. (Pam) Novak and Miss (Jessica) Concannon are to these blessed children. The countless hours that they put into developing curriculum that meets state standards yet is tailored to each child. The numerous hours spent praying with them and teaching them Christ-like behaviors. The significant dollars of their own used to buy students clothes, food, toys, ballet lessons, awards, and more, the increase in love in their own hearts and how that is transferred to the students.

I could also tell you about the amazing volunteers who have come in to love and serve the children. They include the three Michigan-certified teachers who come in to teach computers, music, and art. They also are the people who bring in a lunch for the kids once a week, and those who come in to read and play with the children, the ones who become a mentor for a child.

I could also tell you about the amazing prayer warriors out there. The ones who pray often that God will transform this community through TOL, the people who give sacrificially, on so many occasions, the people who have brought books, supplies, furniture and more. People have donated enough physical supplies to fill my front porch twice!

But, it's really about the kids.

Glory to God!

Aren't they beautiful? Let's just give God a hand a minute for how He has fearfully and wonderfully made these kids.

Now, before I tell you a few stories about the amazing things God is doing in their lives, I want us to reflect on the hardships and struggles many of these kids face. Because sometimes it's just too easy to forget when we hear them singing praises to the Lord with such enthusiasm.

Some have fathers who died this year. Some have multiple half-siblings. Some have fathers who are in prison. Some have fathers who are mentally challenged, absent, or non-existent. Some have mothers who are mentally challenged. Some live in squalor. Some have alcoholic parents. Some have moms with two jobs and some have none. Most receive government assistance. Some live with their relatives, some rent apartments. Some struggle to get enough food, to pay light bills or put gas in their car.

Most sources say that we parent like our parents taught us—right or wrong. And the same is true for many of our families. Poverty can show its face in many ways, but it is primarily a spiritual issue and is often passed on from generation to generation. Did you know that many research groups conclude that if a child grows up in the welfare system, that many have a 75% chance of becoming an adult who depends on the welfare system?

But I won't leave you in the pit.

Did you see the hope in the children's eyes when they sang praises to God? That's the hope of Jesus. That's the peace that passes all understanding.

Kids whose last school year was spent fighting, chasing boys, and playing sick are now excited about learning, enjoying their classmates, and aspiring to be something when they grow up! In October, Izzy invited Jesus into her heart after a class discussion. In January, Harmony did the same. Both have now been baptized right here in this church. They love Jesus and see him working in their lives!

There is research that supports what the Lord is doing in these kids' lives. Did you also know that the Barna Group, a reputable research organization on spiritual matters, did a study that found two out of three Christians accepted Christ before the age of 18, and the younger they accepted Christ the more devoted they were later in life. Do you remember when you accepted Christ? Train a child in the way that they should go and later in life they will not depart from it.

Glory to God!

And that same hope is starting to spread to the parents. Because of what they see in their kids, parents are getting baptized and going to church! Parents are becoming more patient, hopeful, and thankful. People are becoming intimate with Jesus.

Few have questioned the legitimacy of the Holy Spirit's amazing work here. There has been so much fruit produced in so many lives and on so many levels – academically, socially, and spiritually. We believe that TOL is just the beginning, and we have a new challenge in front of us.

Glory to God!

We've made a lot of mistakes starting this school. But I'm going to tell you briefly about the biggest.

When we started, we made two assumptions. First, that the Old Catholic school we were renting would be perfect and would be grandfathered in for all state/city building and fire code. Second, we assumed we didn't have to register with the State since we're a small religious school receiving no state funding.

We were wrong on both accounts. And the state knows we exist. Yet God has stayed the hand of the executioner.

We found all this out a week before we opened our doors. The board unanimously decided to press on as we would try to figure things out.

So for eight months now, we've been praying and searching and deliberating and talking and thinking and trying to discern what the Lord wants us to do so that we can press on to love and serve even more kids.

We found that renovating our current location wasn't even an option as you can't have K/1 on the second floor, and it'd cost hundreds of thousands of dollars for elevators, more fire doors, etc.

We looked at renovating commercial space here and other places in the Edison neighborhood. Most would require $150,000 in renovations, and then you have to pay rent and high utility bills for inefficient buildings. We recently had Matt Challender (of Challender Commercial Real Estate) do a search of commercial properties suitable to our needs in this neighborhood. He was only able to come up with one and said that there really is hardly anything available. And this property is located right on a busy street, is nothing but asphalt, and doesn't meet setbacks for school code— certainly not ideal.

It's not about a building; it's about the kids!

We looked at buying some land – namely the parcels next door and putting portables on it to start. If you can imagine, there is almost no vacant land in this neighborhood. With that, you still have the cost of the land, parking lots, utility hook ups and rent that was nearly quadruple for the same space we have now, and THEY'RE PORTABLES. What kind of message does that send to the community?

It's not about a building; it's about the kids!

We then researched building. We got some builder estimates that said we could build a new energy-efficient building for $100 a square foot. The construction would be much like *a big four bedroom house. And we could raise the whole amount of $500,000 and have no mortgage. We started looking into the land next door and found it suitable for our needs.*

It's not about a building; it's about the kids!

In March, the TOL board unanimously approved us to move forward in developing and raising funds to purchase land and build a small four-classroom school that could house 80-100 kids.

But I think it's even more important to note that ever since we've been in this neighborhood, there has been a spiritual pull to this building and this property. We're not sure exactly why, but so many times in prayer we have known that the building was to be here.

It's not about a building; it's about the kids!

Since we've discerned that this is the direction the Lord is leading us, I need to tell you about some of the miracles that have already taken place.

So far, Mike Seelye has donated 1.1 acres to TOL so that we can swap part of it in trade to make a better parcel, which is right out the windows behind us and to the left.

In addition, the design team that the Lord has brought together has either offered their services for free or for a drastically reduced rate.

Furthermore, this project is even being considered as a fast- build project by Kalamazoo Valley Home Builders Association, where builders from the area unite to build a house or small facility in twenty-four hours that will benefit low income families.

We see the Lord continuing to melt people hearts as they not only think it's a great idea, but they want to get involved. We feel confident at this point that even though the project is estimated at half a million that with all the gifts in kind currently around $50,000 that the total project cost will not be more than $300,000.

It's not about a building; it's about the kids!

If this mission of reaching the lost at an early age and educating them with a Christian worldview is to continue, we need a state-approved building here in the Edison neighborhood – ASAP.

A verse that has been a mantra for me lately has been 1 John 5:14-15. "And we can be confident, that He hears us whenever we ask for anything that is in line with his will. And if he is listening to us, we can be sure that He will give us what we ask for."

Never in my life have I been more confident that this building project for these children you saw today and so many more to come, is HIS WILL.

It's not about a building; it's about the kids!

So for the sake of the children and the future of our community, I'm asking you to turn your eyes towards God and to listen carefully to the Holy Spirit's leading.

There are many ways to get involved with TOL: Prayer, mentoring, volunteering and donating supplies. But tonight, we ask you specifically to listen to what the Spirit is asking you to sacrifice in terms of your finances for these children.

I've been encouraged by many to ask big, so I will. We are asking that an average of $3000 per person be considered *here tonight. We also realize that for some of you, a $300 gift would be a huge sacrifice whereas for others, it would be $30,000. We give glory to God for all sacrificial gifts because we are simply giving back what is already His.*

I challenge end encourage you now. My wife, Amy, and I are part of this as well, and we too have been led by the Spirit to give up a significant portion of our savings to His cause.

It's a miracle every day at Tree of Life. We thank you and give glory to God for you and your families being an integral part of helping make Disciples of Christ that are transforming the world around them!

CHAPTER 12

The Power of Prayer

After my speech at our first banquet, we prayed. People filled out commitment cards and went home. It was such an amazing God- glorifying evening and the presence of the Lord was so thick. Amy and I went out for coffee afterwards and marveled at what God had done. I felt so full that I didn't have any desire to count the money.

The next morning I tallied the money and six month commitments. Was that right? $60,000! Thank you, Jesus! I admit that my flesh was disappointed because it wasn't the full half million needed-- forgive me, Lord! But the Joy triumphed. I began to share the good news. I started asking people if they thought that was good. They asked me if I were crazy and told me it was miraculous. Again I claimed ignorance since I had never done anything like that before.

I knew that at least one more mountain range was moved.

Then He sent Ken...

I knew Ken as one of the sound/video guys at Centerpoint when I was part of their Worship team. I didn't know he was a builder until he called me one day. He wanted to meet for breakfast and talk about this school building project.

I shared several stories about what God was doing in the life of kids. Ken eventually said, "Well, I'm supposed to build your school. I watched the video on your website and even had my wife Kathy come in and take a look. I told her the same and asked her if it was okay. She said, yes."

I told him that we had $30,000 in cash and $30,000 in commitments over the next six months. We were convicted not to take out any loans, assuming no one in their right mind would lend us money anyway. We planned to build until we ran out of money. If God wanted this done then He would have to figure out how to do it. Ken said, okay and that $30,000 might buy us a foundation. The realities of our world are rarely encouraging. As we talked further, I graciously accepted his offer.

Ken took over the project. I didn't realize how that would work, but found out quickly I wasn't supposed to do anything unless he asked me to. When Ken said jump, I jumped. He was a real Godsend. Another mountain range was moved. He was well connected in the community and quickly got the word out. As Ken talked with contractors, they also asked about our budget. Ken would reply, "We don't have a budget. But we believe that whatever you bill us for, the Lord will provide."

A Seedling - Planning Commission Meeting Invitation

"On July 7, at 7 p.m., Tree of Life will be presenting our site plan before the City of Kalamazoo at City Hall. This is an important meeting, as we must gain their approval in order to build the new school. I ask that you claim Joshua Chapter 1 with me: "Wherever you set foot, you will be on land I have given you. No one will be able to stand against you as long as you live. For I will be with you as I was with Moses. I will not fail you or abandon you."

Furthermore, the Planning Commission will hear all people who are FOR or AGAINST this. There are some who will show up opposed to this. We need to rally our troops and have people speak up who are in favor of what Tree of Life is offering the community. If you feel led to share how Tree of Life is a benefit to the community, please come to City Hall on July 7. If you are unable to attend, please sign a written statement and send it to me."

After we went public with the building project, we, of course, were looking for any place that might help us. I knew that Keith was on the board of Christ Followers for Change (CFC). They were a coalition of churches joined together to partner with Kalamazoo ministries and those in Africa. Their goal was to bring about systemic change primarily about poverty and education. They would prayerfully select ministries, promote them in their churches and then take a one-time offering around Thanksgiving.

I asked Keith if I should talk to them about Tree of Life. He said that he wasn't sure if we would be something that they were interested in but provided me an opportunity to speak before their board. I arrived at the meeting, noticing that I was last on the agenda. I heard their meetings only lasted an hour. With fifteen minutes remaining, they were on agenda item two. I was number four. The hour ended as they just finished item two. They called for a fifteen-minute extension; agenda item three took ten of those. With five minutes left, I was told to speak. My head was spinning. I said a quick prayer and talked fast. I figured my chances of selling Tree of Life to the CFC board were slim to none. Keith called later and said that the CFC board wanted more information. I wrote the following informational proposal.

Tree of Life School Building Project

- *TOL is building an approximate 5,000 sq. ft. building at 2001 Cameron St. in the Edison Neighborhood of Kalamazoo. There will be four classrooms, one office, four bathrooms, and two large storage areas. It is a stick built structure, with hardboard siding, and a shingle roof. The 1.34 acres is owned by TOL. The school building plans meet all state building and fire codes. Ken Klok of the Kalamazoo Valley Homebuilders Association is the construction project manager. The site plan has been approved by the city of Kalamazoo. We are anticipating 25 students this year. The building can accommodate 80-100 students.*
- *Without this building, we can no longer continue our mission. ALL schools in the state of Michigan must have a facility that meets all building and fire codes for a school. We are committed to the Edison neighborhood, and there are no existing buildings that meet all codes. We wholeheartedly believe that this is just the beginning of TOL and not the end.*
- *Renewing young minds and transforming young lives is the vision of TOL. Not only has the good news of Jesus Christ been spread to so many children and families, but we have been able to help and equip families with tools and support to help break the cycle of poverty. Every day at TOL, we lead students in praise and worship, academic excellence, and how to live as Disciples of Christ. We also empower and engage parents to make wise life choices. It truly is a miracle every day at TOL.*
- *TOL fits perfectly with CFC's mission in changing the world by the gospel of Christ through education. 180 days a year, 5 days a week, Jesus is proclaimed Lord of all at TOL! Students are trained in the way they should go as we set high academic, social, and spiritual goals for each child. We believe God's vision for TOL has the power to change and transform not only the Edison neighborhood, but all of*

Kalamazoo and beyond. It already has, for there are 1000's of people around this continent praying for all the people involved.

- Another unique aspect TOL has to offer is vast opportunities for hands-on activity from all the local churches that are a part of CFC. While many may not be able to go to Africa, anyone can come and be a part of the TOL family. Last year, we had about 20 volunteers from Kalamazoo who helped make TOL such an amazing experience. As we double the number of students this year, we can at least double the number of volunteers needed to love and serve the families at TOL! Furthermore, we hope to engage even more people in the building of the new school.

- The project is estimated at $500,000. We have had over $200,000 in cash, commitments, and gifts in kind already. We are asking CFC for 10% of the project cost which is $50,000. This is a one-time commitment. We will build as we have the money. We will not be taking out any long-term loans. We may take out short-term loans based on solid commitments such as one from CFC. We currently have about $60,000 in cash and $40,000 in commitments to be filled by the end of the year.

- Currently, the land is held by TOL Holdings, LLC. The TOL entity is organized as a ministry under Vanguard Church right now. In September, we will begin the process to organize as a 501(c) (3) Educational institution. In order to become one, you must have a state compliant building. That is why we have not done so yet. By January, we hope to be in our new building, organized as a 501(c) (3) educational institution, and standing on our own.

- There is room to expand on the property with another 4 classrooms. We won't be stepping into that phase for another three years.

- For this school year, we have an operational budget of $125,000. Currently, we are paying about $1000 a month in rent, utilities, etc. at St. Joe's. We do not anticipate our costs to increase with the new building, as we pay no taxes, the building is paid for, and is energy efficient. The Lord has provided all our operational expenses to date!

- We are seeking additional sources of funding from the Greg Jennings Foundation, other foundations, individuals, and organizations. We are praying that the Lord leads us to the right people. We are also *expecting many more significant donations in the actual construction of the project as excitement in the community grows and the Spirit moves.*

- *I believe that we are sustainable by His power and Grace. First of all, I must be clear in letting you know that this wasn't my idea. The Lord came to me with this. This is His vision. It took me five years to accept the call. He has proven faithful time and time again. It stuns me that in just over a year, the Lord has brought in over $300,000 in cash, commitments, gifts in kind for the kids of Edison! I have never in my life done any fundraising or had the desire to it. I pray every day that I do not get in the way. I am confident that TOL School is His will! And I think that there is already one principal, five teachers, 20 volunteers, 25 kids, 15 families, and 1000's of supporters in this community who would agree.*

Thank you so much for your time, prayers, and consideration. Praise God for all the good things being accomplished through CFC!

In Christ,

Adam Sterenberg

Principal

Tree of Life

www.tolschool.org

One hot sweaty night at vacation Bible school Keith asked me how much should we ask from CFC. I rather casually said $50,000. He gave me a look and said, okay. A month later, the CFC board approved our project for $50,000. Praise God for another mountain range moved!

***

As doors continued to open for the school, it became evident that we truly had a purpose for our community and the students we served. One family in particular saw how much we loved them after an explosion in their home. According to an article on the WOOD TV station:

Published: Tuesday, 07 Jun 2011, 3:19 AM EDT

KALAMAZOO, Mich. (WOOD) - A man suffered severe burns after a methamphetamine lab exploded in the basement of his home.

When rescue personnel arrived, they saw the man lying in the street. They tended to his injuries and extinguished the blaze, which was contained to the basement of the home.

That was home to one of our school families. When a meth lab is discovered in a home the entire contents are immediately condemned. Praise God, the TOL family immediately sprang into action. My family housed the student and her family while others provided new clothes, food and eventually a new place to live.

Later I wrote:

Thank you so much for all your prayers, clothing, furniture etc. for the family! God has revealed a place right down our street that we hope to close on this week. In fact, on Monday at 6 p.m., we will be cleaning the house and trimming the overgrowth. If you are interested in helping, let me know. Pray that this deal goes through and that they are moved in this week. Once the deal is closed, I'll let everyone know where you can drop off clothing and furniture. As (the mother) has already said, "I don't know what I would have done without you!" The family is experiencing the unconditional love of the body of Christ.

A Seedling - 11th Wedding Anniversary

On July 7, 2011 we were at a cottage in Silver Lake with my parent's whole family. For one whole week we enjoyed the sun, water, dunes and cherry strudel. But on this wedding anniversary, instead of going out for dinner and renting scooters, Amy and I drove two hours to Kalamazoo City Hall. There was an approval meeting for our plan to build Tree of Life School - the newest school in Edison in almost 100 years.

This was a potential deal breaker. If we didn't get this, we were done. We knew there would be naysayers present so we invited people to come and speak on our behalf. About twenty-five supporters showed up and gave testimony to the great things God was doing for our community through Tree of Life. After twenty minutes of testimonies the council voted unanimously to approve building Tree of Life School!

Glory to God for another mountain range moved!

TOL Quick Facts 2011

- 25 Students in grades PreK-5
- 75% of students are minorities
- One principal, two teachers, part time music teacher, many, many volunteers
- $125,000 annual budget. 90% met by donations. 10% met by parent's tuition.
- Renting two classrooms at St. Joseph's Catholic Church.
- 50% of TOL families have a single mom as head of the household
- 75% of TOL families are on some form of government assistance
- 50% live or have lived in the Edison neighborhood
- 50% of TOL kids have little or no church connection
- $18,000 average income for TOL families
- Verse of the Year - "Your word is a lamp to guide my feet and a light for my path." Psalm 119:105

CHAPTER 13

The Difference

Our school was different in so many ways. Jesus was at the forefront of everything. We worshipped differently. Prayed differently. We needed the Lord to provide 90% of our budget. Nobody knew about us so we had to go door to door and recruit our families in places I never thought I would go.

Over the past few years I had gotten to know Stephanie at the shelter. She was the director of the preschool program. She was an amazing woman of God with a huge heart for kids. She called me before the start of our second school year because she had two families she wanted to recommend to enroll in our school. Because we weren't a legal school yet, we didn't receive busing assistance from Kalamazoo Public Schools. Stephanie figured they could use a shelter van to drive kids to school.

I went one morning to meet two sets of potential parents. Another single mom named Alice "crashed" our meeting. Even though Stephanie didn't recommend her, I was okay with her staying. We had a great meeting, and I answered all of their questions. Alice hung around to talk with me personally. She began to share her story of drug abuse, losing her kids to the State a second time and coming to the shelter to turn her life around. She had hit rock bottom and was desperate to do right. She wanted her kids to be part of a school that honored God. She was serious. I could hear it in her voice.

It was a joy to watch Alice and her children grow immensely in the Lord. The kids had become on fire for Jesus. Alice gave a powerful testimony at our second TOL fundraiser dinner.

I met Josh and Sarah at the same meeting I met Alice. Josh and Sarah struggled with drug addiction. They gave their lives to the Lord and voluntarily left their home in Portage and checked into the shelter. They heard about our school through Stephanie, whose daughter attended our school. They were pretty sure that God wanted their girls to attend a Christian school, but the money was just not in the budget. Josh told Sarah to have faith and give it another day. The next day Josh received notification in the mail that he no longer owed money on a certain debt. The amount was exactly the same as what their payments would be for Tree of Life. They were overjoyed and took this as a clear sign to send the girls to our school.

A Seedling - Treasure Hunt
June 18th, 2010

Easter is a sacred and holy day on which we celebrate the resurrection of our Lord and Savior Jesus Christ. Many of us celebrate by going to church and pouring out our souls in praise and worship to the King. And later, many of us celebrate this sacred and holy holiday by hiding a bunch of pastel-colored plastic eggs filled with candy, money and other things to help our children understand the true meaning of Easter. Huh?

For several years now I have watched my kids and their cousins become so excited over the celebration of Easter—the great hunt for the treasure in plastic eggs. While the adults go out and hide all the eggs the anticipation builds among the kids. When we finally come back inside and get out their bags to collect the treasure, they are nearly bursting at the seams with excitement.

We give them the signal to start and laugh as we see the joy on their faces as they go tearing out into the yard looking for these plastic eggs. They are not satisfied with one; they keep moving and running all over until we finally tell them to stop.

A treasure hunt is exciting because the kids are running around looking for good things that are hidden. They know the eggs are out there, and they know that there are treats inside. It's also exciting because they're not quite sure what they're going to get. They know that the treasure could be ANYWHERE. If they don't find it in one place, they don't stop and sulk and ponder, 'Why on EARTH is it not here? Did I do something wrong?' They just keep right on looking in the next spot.

These thoughts ran through my mind a couple of days ago when I was thanking God for the releasing of funds for Tree of Life. He led me on my own treasure hunt through his word regarding the word treasure. Here's what I found.

"The Kingdom of Heaven is like a treasure that a man discovered hidden in a field. In his excitement, he hid it again and sold everything he owned to get enough money to buy the field." Matthew 13:44

"Don't store up treasures here on earth, where moths eat them and rust destroys them, and where thieves break in and steal. Store your treasures in heaven, where moths and rust cannot destroy, and thieves do not break in and steal. Wherever your treasure is, there the desires of your heart will also be." Matthew 6:19-21

"Teach those who are rich in this world not to be proud and not to trust in their money, which is so unreliable. Their trust should be in God, who richly gives us all we need for our enjoyment. Tell them to use their money to do good. They should be rich in good works and generous to those in need,

always being ready to share with others. By doing this they will be storing up their treasure as a good foundation for the future so that they may experience true life." 1 Timothy 6:16-19

"Tune your ears to wisdom, and concentrate on understanding. Cry out for insight, and ask for understanding. Search for them as you would for silver; seek them like hidden treasures. Then you will understand what it means to fear the Lord, and you will gain knowledge of God." Proverbs 2:2-5

The Spirit has convicted me that right now we are on a treasure hunt. God wants us to run with excitement from hiding place to hiding place looking for the treasure. He doesn't want us to stop and worry when the treasure is not where we looked or where we thought it should be. He just wants us to keep running and looking with excitement because he has already given us the field and has promised that the treasure is there.

"Seek the Kingdom of God above all else, and live righteously, and he will give you everything you need." My spirit is convicted of this, but my flesh is still terrified at times. Please pray that our spirits are able to silence the flesh.

Money is one of the treasures we're looking for. Praise God for the almost forty individuals and their families who have given more than $14,000. It has been such a joy to hear and see people saying, "I believe!" We look forward with great anticipation to how the Lord will fulfill our yearly need of $125,000. However, money is only a minor treasure compared to the great find we are in search of.

"Suppose a woman has ten silver coins and loses one. Won't she light a lamp and sweep the entire house and search carefully until she finds it? And when she finds it, she will call in her friends and neighbors and say, 'Rejoice with me

because I have found my lost coin.' In the same way, there is joy in the presence of God's angels when even one sinner repents." Luke 15:8-10

Kids and families are the true treasure! Money will someday pass away, but souls of God's children are forever. Please pray and lift up the Street Bosses and their teams as they go out in the field and search for the greatest treasure of all, the students whose lives are going to be transformed by the power of Jesus Christ.

Please pray for us as we continue to search for all of the hidden treasures. Please pray that we have joy in enthusiasm as we gather in all the students who desire to be a part of Tree of Life. Please pray for joy and enthusiasm as we continue the hunt for generous people who have been called to support Tree of Life.

I still don't know what finding plastic eggs filled with candy has to do with Easter, but I'm sure glad the Spirit used it for His glory in transforming the way I think. May He transform you as well!

A Seedling - "Hairrifying" Fundraiser
Published in Community Voices by Sonya Hollins

Withee, a Kalamazoo native, plans to raise $500 by promising to shave his beard and hair for Tree of Life Elementary School. He has been able to grow a full beard since his sophomore year of high school. He hadn't cut his hair in a year and wanted to let it all go for a good cause.

"I came up with the idea about a month ago. My friends and parents always said I looked better with shorter hair so I might as well make use of all my hair," said Withee who resides at the Western campus ministry, His House.

"Growing up in Christian schools was a big motivation for me. I know the school (Tree of Life) needs a lot of support right now," said Withee.

Tree of Life Christian Elementary School is currently renting space for its K-5th graders from St. Joseph Catholic Church, 936 Lake St. in Kalamazoo. Adam Sterenberg founded the school in 2010 after being led by God to start a Christian school on Kalamazoo's south side. The school has more than two-dozen students, however will expand in the fall of 2012 when their new school building is complete.

Students attend the Christian school for only 5% of their family's income used as tuition. The new building will be on the property adjacent to their fiduciary agent, Vanguard Ministries (an offspring of Center Point Ministries). Generous donations of funds, labor, and materials are making Sterenberg's vision a reality faster than he ever imagined. More funding is needed, however, to complete the building and assist in other operating expenses.

Withee has already reached about $200 and hopes to eventually meet his goal of $500 by Valentine's Day. He encourages the public to join in and add anything they can to the effort.

"It is hard to raise money because I am only asking Western students as of right now. It is a little hard getting money from students," Withee said.

If Withee succeeds, he plans to cut off all his hair in front of the children who attend Tree of Life school while being videotaped and later the video will be posted online."

Praise God! The WMU students and TOL family raised a total of $2,321!

On Tuesday, March 27, 2012, we took the upper grades to Lansing to see the Capitol and the Michigan Historical Museum. They were so well behaved as the learned about our state and where many decisions that affect all of us come from.

But even more amazing than the Capitol, museum and the Michigan State University Dairy Store was what I got to witness in the van on the way up. Three of the girls had their Bibles along and were sharing their favorite verses with each other. They also gave me suggestions on what the next verse of the week should be. I took one of their suggestions for that week's verse. *"Don't let anyone think less of you because you are young. Be an example to all believers in what you say, in the way you live, in your love, your faith, and your purity"* (1 Timothy 4:12).

A Seedling - $30,000 Prayer?
Tuesday, May 15ᵗʰ, 2012

In October of 2011, we started praying for a third full time teacher. We've also been praying that the Lord might bless the current staff with some raises. I had been sensing about $1,500 per person.

At Christmas time, we received a single $30,000 donation. I had never talked to these people. I had never sent them any information about us. In fact, when I met the person, they told me they had the check made out to another organization. They went to drop it off, but the organization was closed. So, he tore up the check and wrote a new check to TOL. I laughed!

New teacher at TOL= $25,000.

Raises for the staff = $4,500.

Power of the Holy Spirit = Priceless!

The Lord continued to move in powerful ways. So many things were happening that were far greater than we could ever dare or imagine. And then a very special day came, a day that I thought impossible.

A Seedling - Ground Breaking

As we thanked God for the lives we were changing, we couldn't help but thank Him for the journey we were about to embark on with a new building. We thought it was important to further dedicate the land for God's glory. On October 18, 2011, we had the TOL groundbreaking ceremony. It looked like it would rain that day, but it held off. The land was cleared and the corners of the building were staked. My wife, Amy, created a glass mosaic tree of life to be placed in the finished building. About one hundred people showed up —parents, children and supporters. We lifted up heart-felt prayers and had people sign a sheet to be put in a Bible that would be buried under the building.

Kim attained silver shovels so we could "officially" break ground. Ken and I dug the first scoops, but we then let everyone dig. This building belonged to God and we were all part of it.

I met a guy named Dave from Chicago. When I asked him if he was in town for something, he told me he drove out special just for this. He said he felt sick earlier and almost didn't make it. He always grew excited when a new urban Christian school started. It was an incredible blessing and honor!

CHAPTER 14

Dependence Day

"So if the Son sets you free, you are truly free" (John 8:36).

I had never been more dependent in my life than I was at the time the school was being completed– dependent on God that is. I depended on the Lord for clean air, food, shelter and clothing. But I depended on Him for joy, peace and love as well. His goodness to me is unexplainable.

I was depending on God for the safety and prosperity of the Tree of Life kids over the summer. I was depending on Him completing a first-class facility for the kids in less than forty-five days. I was depending on Him to provide the remaining monies of this $500,000 project. I was depending on Him to raise new students and families who would be joining us in the fall. I was depending on praying people to lift up all our needs and that people's hearts would melt and be obedient to the Holy Spirit.

Because of my dependability on God, I can tell you that I had never been freer and more alive than at that time. It was so hard to give up my independence. But by becoming more dependent I had been given gifts that were far greater. I wouldn't trade them for anything.

The time came to pour footings and the foundation slab. We figured that would eat up most of our cash on hand. The first bill came. But, to my shock, enclosed with the bill was a check from the company for the exact amount. Dumbfounded, I asked Ken about it. He told me that they wanted to donate the concrete, and that was the best way for them to do it. Every time a bill came, there was another check enclosed. The concrete finishing crew never sent us a bill either. In the end, there was over $30,000 in concrete and finish work donated. Did this count as one or two mountain ranges?

One day a guy named Jim walked up to the school and talked with Ken. He asked if we had anyone to do the roof. Ken said no. Jim said he wanted to do it at no charge. In fact, he was going to call his brother-in-law and try to get him to donate the shingles. The entire roof, labor and materials, was donated. Another mountain range moved!

A Seedling - Prayer Studs

On Friday, January 3, TOL students, family and friends went to the new school to write prayers and scripture on the studs. We gathered inside and prayed. I expressed to the kids, "This brand new school is just a small taste of how much Jesus loves you. He's building this for YOU!" As soon as I said that, several kindergartners started to bounce and squeal with huge smiles on their faces. Glory to God!

The 50 people there went around finding places on the studs or floor to write and draw. It was incredible to witness. There was such joy and anticipation even though it was so cold! I went back a few days later to take a picture of each verse, prayer, or drawing. It took me over two hours!

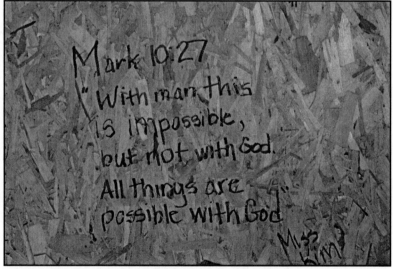

Before I had too long to think about it, a friend contacted me about used office furniture. They were remodeling their car dealership and wanted to know if I could use anything. I saw that it was gently used high quality furniture made from solid cherry wood, high-grade metal and fabrics. All I had to do was pick out what I wanted, and they would store it and install it when I was ready.

A Seedling - TOL Building Update
Thursday, January 26, 2012

Our God is so amazing! It is so amazing to see God bring so many people together to bring His Vision to life! Praise God for the overwhelming amount of work and materials that have been donated! Here's a summary:

Face Value of total building project: $500,000

Approximate Value of Property, Material, & Labor SO FAR: $250,000

Approximate Paid Expenses so far: $50,000

Approximate Cash currently on hand for building: $100,000

So, as one friend puts it, the Lord has done a $250,000 project so far for $50,000. The list of individuals and businesses that are generously giving is so long already. I do want to specifically praise God for Ken Klok, our project manager with a big heart, who has put in countless hours working and organizing people to create what you see.

It's hard to estimate when the project will be done or how much more it will cost. We do know that it will be done in His perfect timing and through His perfect provision. Ken says it could be as early as March but for sure before school starts in the fall. Please pray that all workers, donors, and

*supporters will be incredibly blessed as this project will bless
our community for generations to come.*

*I drove one of our students by yesterday and asked if she knew
what that building was. She said no and I told her it was the
new Tree of Life school. She said, "Wooooooahh!! That's our
new school??" And then I told her that's just a small example
of how much Jesus loves you!*

We thank God!

Ken and I both got quotes for the flooring of the school. We needed
5,000-square-feet of commercial grade vinyl tile. It was amazing to see
both companies try so hard to give their absolute lowest price for God's
glory. The entire school building was beautifully tiled and carpeted for $1
per square foot installed.

One morning while driving two of our students, brothers Eric and
Damarquez, in from the eastside, I asked them if they were excited about
the new school being built. Damarquez asked if we could drive by it.
School started over an hour ago, but I decided to take them anyway. As

we drove up to the new school, they exclaimed, "Whoa! Is that the new school?"

The bricklayers were working hard. We got out and I showed them around. While watching the bricklayers a minute, one of the workers asked them if they wanted to lay a brick. They could hardly contain their excitement as they crawled onto the scaffolding to place a brick. It was powerful. A year later they still point to the exact spot and say, "That's where my brick is, Mr. S." And I tell them that they will always be part of Tree of Life.

One day I came by the worksite, and Ken was cutting the siding for the peaks and soffits. I was surprised because it was aluminum rather than vinyl. "That looks like pretty nice stuff, Ken." He said, "It's about the best money can buy." The local salesman called the owner of the company in Grand Rapids and described the Tree of Life building project. The owner was happy to donate all the siding. Another mountain range moved.

We had our second fundraising dinner in May of 2012. All the money went towards finishing the new school building. It was another beautiful evening, and we had a packed house. God was definitely present. The kids sang, parents gave testimonies, and we asked people to once again give sacrificially. Someone in attendance called Ken and said that he would donate every interior door for the school...sixteen gorgeous solid wood-core doors.

A crew drove in several times from Grand Rapids. They were all part of the one large family. They hung all the drywall for free. Another family member paid for all the materials. Another mountain range moved.

Just days before school opened, we received one large "L-shaped" desk for me, one smaller "L-shaped" desk set for an administrative assistant, two large wood file cabinets, six office chairs, a comfy hospitality chair and six guest chairs.

Things like that continued to manifest. Ken asked me to find a concrete well for a parking lot drain. I went to a company in town, stopped in the office and introduced myself. I told him a little about our school and asked to whom I should give the information packet. He said that would probably be him since he was the owner. After talking with him for a bit, he said he could help us out. They later delivered a drain...but a bill was never sent.

A couple of local painting companies agreed to paint the school. They talked to Sherwin Williams' representative and asked if they could demo over eighty gallons of paint. They agreed, and all the paint for school was donated. The painters never sent us a bill.

I had been asking God, ""What are we going to do for a play set, Lord? We really need something." In June of 2012, my family went camping at PJ Hoffmaster in Muskegon. One night we went out with our friends to the Whippy Dip for ice cream. When we pulled up, I was drawn to the play set. There were three big swings, a rope swing, a tire swing, a straight slide, and a snaked tube slide, climbing wall, rope ladder and canopied upper deck. It had so much to do in a relatively compact space.

A bunch of boys from a little league team piled out of a van and ran to the play set. They gave it a real work out. When I finished my ice cream, I inspected the set to see if there was a manufacturer's name anywhere. On the back I found a large metal plate that read Rainbow Play Structures. I googled Rainbow Play Structures and found a dealer in Paw Paw, not far from town. I asked if they had put up the one at the Whippy Dip. When they confirmed, I asked about having the same model at our school.

The guy told me, "Well, you know what, the owner just put up one like that in his yard last year, and he's trying to get rid of it."

I emphasized, "Well, I don't want one like it, I want that EXACT model."

"Yes. It's that EXACT model," he said.

I was stunned. The owner was asking $5,500 installed. I asked if he could do better for our school, and he said he would do it for $5,000. That sounded like a good deal, and I told him I would pray about it.

I later emailed him for the price of a brand new set. He replied that a new one in the box is $12,000. I called back and told him we would love the used one. It was exactly what we needed. The kids absolutely loved it.

In June of 2012, the building was getting closer to being done. I started thinking about furniture and finish items. I would have been happy to find some used classroom furniture. But when I talked to Ken about it he challenged me, "We're building these kids a first-class facility. Are you going to put a bunch of used and ratty furniture in here?" Ken's words convicted me. I prayed about it and then sent out the following letter:

God is challenging me again. When I saw the brick going up on the new building, it made two impressions. First is that TOL is here to stay. The second is HIS KIDS ARE WORTH IT!

We have less than two months to go before teachers will begin setting up their classrooms for the fall! We need the Lord to perform many more miracles so that the school can be completed on schedule. Please pray with us!

There are many large bills to come and our building fund is quickly disappearing. Besides landscaping, sixty trees, parking lots, sidewalks, and a driveway, there are also many elements that are necessary to the learning and development of the children.

God has challenged me to ask boldly for a building full of new furniture, technology, and supplies. I'm amazed at how expensive things are, but we are as always trusting that God will provide and HE WILL BE GLORIFIED!

In the letter was the cost breakdown of every item– tables, chairs, teacher desks, white boards, activity tables, sinks, toilets, smart projectors, laptops and an outdoor play structure. We asked people to "buy what they could" off the list. The list totaled $35,000.

God confirmed Ken's words. Within in one week we had $35,000!

Every person, every contractor, every laborer, every company gave sacrificially. There were so many who gave that I didn't even know about. The end result is that God moved through people to create an $800,000 school for $300,000. He moved 35 mountain ranges to build the Tree of Life School in less than two years. And even more importantly, he built everyone's faith immensely!

TOL Quick Facts 2012

- 40 Students in grades PreK-5
- 75% of students are minorities
- One principal, three teachers, part time music teacher, many, many volunteers
- 1st year in brand new 5,000 square foot first class facility. 3rd newest commercial building in Edison in over 30 years.
- $150,000 annual budget. 90% met by donations. 10% met by parent's tuition.
- 50% of TOL families have a single mom as head of the household
- 75% of TOL families are on some form of government assistance
- 50% live or have lived in the Edison Neighborhood
- 50% of TOL kids have little or no church connection
- $18,000 average income for TOL families
- Verse of the Year - "Teach me your ways, O Lord, that I may live according to your truth! Grant me purity of heart, so that I may honor you. With all my heart I will praise you, O Lord my God. I will give glory to your name forever, for your love for me is very great" (Psalm 86:11-13).

CHAPTER 15

First Day of School

"And the word became flesh"

It was beautiful. It was surreal. It was supernatural. We had a first-class state-of-the-arts building that was worth more than $500,000 for the kids of Edison. It had three-color brick, the best aluminum siding, beautiful wood-cased windows and dozens of new trees, bushes and shrubs. We also had a highly visible illuminated sign, glass entry way and a super fun play set.

Those who came onto our campus drove across the fresh concrete and asphalt and walked into an inviting atmosphere in the school where the floors had beautiful neutral-colored tiled flooring with bursts of color. The walls were a Khaki and soft green accent throughout which perfectly allowed the accent of the solid wood doors, wood cabinets and sinks in each classroom stand out. Each room contained quality furniture, desks, and smart projectors. Those who visited said they felt as if they were walking into a home more than a school…and that's exactly what we were hoping for.

There were so many firsts. The first thing we all said was, "It's so peaceful!" Everything was so beautiful, shiny, exciting. We added Anne, our first new full-time teacher since we started, and for the first time I had an office instead of working from home.

And then the first day at the new school came. We had excited parents and students pull up in our very own driveway and walk down our brand new sidewalk as opposed to the shared driveway of St. Joseph Church and a climb to the second level space we once rented. We had five school busses pull up and drop off kids, as opposed to parents helping me carpool students to class. We had forty beautiful children enrolled, which was the most we had ever had. It was overwhelming. Even a newspaper reporter showed up.

We decided that we would hold our all school worship times in the commons––the hallway. We came together and sang with more enthusiasm than ever before! The kids were so excited to be experiencing the new school that God built for them. We gave glory to God for building us a new school.

Thank you, Jesus, thank you!

On the second day of school, the *Kalamazoo Gazette* sent a photographer/reporter named Mark. He took pictures of kids coming to school and getting off the bus as I was busy welcoming them back to school. When things died down, Mark asked me where we got the money to build this. I replied, "The Lord. I'm sorry if that sounds cliché, but if somebody can give me a better explanation, I'm willing to hear it."

He came inside and stayed for our time of worship in song. He even took a close-up photo of the sheet that had our verse of the year from Psalms 86:11-13 that he posted on the Mlive.com article.

After worship, he took some more pictures and just wandered around. He asked me to sit down to identify the students he had photographed. I started sharing with him the innumerable miracles that occurred with building of this school and could see that he was genuinely mystified. When I had finished he said, "That is one of the most genuine God stories I have ever heard." I rejoiced in my heart.

A few days later I ran into Keith and happened to mention Mark's visit. Keith knew him personally and promptly told me that he was a staunch atheist. I rejoiced out loud this time! I am constantly amazed when people are transformed by encountering the living God!

Even as I reflect on the story of the Tree of Life School, I realize that it wasn't a cakewalk. Along with all those new and exciting "firsts" came a hundred more situations that required a lot of work. I had been a dishwasher and janitor. I had been a bus driver and emergency shelter. So, when the new school was built and questions of lawn and snow removal were asked, it was assumed I would take care of it. But again, thanks to Jesus and His awesomeness, He sent a community person our way who offered to do both for free!

I had hoped that the place would only need to be swept, mopped and have garbage taken out every other day while school was in session. But, when the first half day of school ended, it was brutally obvious that the school, with only forty students, needed to be cleaned each night. It was not beneath me to do it, but I needed to organize parent volunteers. Within a week, we had all the days covered.

Many of those who had come to Tree of Life stayed with us; however, more than half of our families were new. Not only did that mean getting to know a lot more families, it also meant that the needs of our families increased dramatically. We had to step up our game with loving and serving each other. We also needed more volunteers for recess and lunchroom duty.

A Seedling - Prayer Caves
September 2012 by Jessica

Our second day of school the 3rd-5th graders learned how to make a "prayer cave." Students get down on their knees, fold themselves in half, and put their hands over their head. This helps students stay focused and block out distractions as they pray. We talked about how this is our special way to pray to talk to God, hear His voice and see what He wants to show us. One of our new students in our class was so excited about the prayer cave that he exclaimed, "Wow, God is telling me and showing me so much! Can I go into my prayer cave anytime I want?" It was incredible to see his enthusiasm to hear from God!

CHAPTER 16

Getting Sucked In

As our building project was coming to completion, we could see how far God had brought us. We had more students than the twelve original "disciples." And now, we would be able to add to our staff with a new teacher.

Annie grew up in Holland, Michigan and attended the local Christian schools. After graduating from Hope College, she took a teaching job at Rehoboth Christian School in New Mexico just outside the Navajo and Zuni reservation. She thoroughly enjoyed her teaching ministry; however, after two years her desire was to move back to Michigan to be closer to family. She felt called to continue her ministry in a diverse Christian school and saw our job posting as the perfect opportunity.

When she didn't get a reply from us right away, she applied to other places. She still felt that Tree of Life was for her even though we paid so much less than her other prospective positions. She later shared that the three months she spent waiting and questioning her job options were terrible, and she felt immediate peace upon accepting us. Annie is an incredible teacher and has grown in her gifts from the Spirit, relationship with Jesus, prayer life and prophecy. She said one reason God wanted her to take the job at Tree of Life was for her own spiritual growth.

Through all of our growing pains, we prayed that the Holy Spirit would continue to move in power in the lives of TOL families. We prayed that Jesus would save those who were lost. We prayed that Jesus would be our Joy every day. We prayed that demons would flee from the light of Christ that was prevalent in so many of our kids and families. We prayed that TOL would become a center of healing, and we would live into our key verse of Revelation 22:2. We prayed we would become more intimate with Christ every day, and that these children would soon lead us even deeper into the Kingdom.

> *Then the angel showed me the river of the water of life, as clear as crystal, flowing from the throne of God and of the Lamb down the middle of the great street of the city. On each side of the river stood the tree of life, bearing twelve crops of fruit, yielding its fruit every month. And the leaves of the tree are for the healing of the nations. No longer will there be any curse. The throne of God and of the Lamb will be in the city, and his servants will serve him. They will see his face, and his name will be on their foreheads. There will be no more night. They will not need the light of a lamp or the light of the sun, for the Lord God will give them light. And they will reign forever and ever (Revelation 22:1-5).*

As we prayed, we were given those like Talanja. She and her three children moved from the Chicago projects to Kalamazoo and quickly joined Vanguard Church where she met Jonathan whom she later married.

In 2011, she came to a school family potluck with a friend from church. She really had no idea what we were all about. At this point in time she had a bad taste in her mouth about kids and education. She had recently lost her job as a teacher's aide and was bitter with the school system. At the end of the potluck, the twelve students sang praise and worship songs. Talanja later said, "I started crying. I didn't even know why. I'm like, what's going on here? This isn't even a real school; they don't even have enough kids to fill one class. These aren't even my kids!"

Later in the year she volunteered to be a server at our fundraising dinner. As she was serving, she kept hearing bits and pieces of testimonies. Soon she was completely sucked in and stopped serving altogether. She pulled up a chair and just listened to what the Lord was doing at our school.

That summer (2012) she came walking by the unfinished new school building. I was standing by the temporary sign when she expressed how she really wanted to get involved at our school. I told her we really didn't have any paid positions, but we always needed volunteers. She agreed to volunteer three days a week, six hours a day.

She showed up the first day of school and was truly amazing. She did everything well—answered phones, filed papers, took kids out for recess, subbed, gave kids literacy lessons and even helped keep them in order. She was such a Godsend. While we did not budget for an assistant, the Lord kept pressing on my heart to pay her. I went from giving her gratuities to putting her on the payroll for six hours a week. But as the next year came, we budgeted to pay her for all the hours she worked.

In our third year, we really felt that God wanted each kid to have a mentor. It would be like Big Brothers/Big Sisters but with a Jesus focus. We wanted the mentors to build a relationship with the kids by spending a minimum of five hours a month with them outside of school.

God connected me with Pastor Mark in the spring of 2012. He was the campus pastor at Solid Grounds. He had a group of hockey players who were in the process of helping our friends fix up their house in Edison. I told him a little about us and about what God was doing. He seemed interested and wanted to have lunch together to talk more. At lunch he inquired about how the students in their campus ministry might get involved. I mentioned that God wanted each kid to have a mentor.

I had no idea Mark was tenacious as a pit bull. When we finally started in September, Mark was chasing me down in his excitement to connect his students with ours. Working through my new duties and new responsibilities that came with the new school building was overwhelming. Mark took the reins and called me a couple times a week to set up meetings with mentors, mentees and parents until every kid who wanted a mentor got one, and most of them got two. The students and mentors of the Bronco Buddies program would meet once a month for a special event at Solid Grounds. Whether it was a swim party at the university pool or attending a ball game, it was really special.

CHAPTER 17

Leaves

"And the leaves were for the healing of the nations..." (Revelation 22:2).

Before moving to Kalamazoo, Jessica didn't really believe much in healing. She believed God would eventually heal someone if you prayed long enough. She knew Jesus healed many people in the Bible right on the spot. However, she had never been exposed to people laying on hands and being instantly healed.

When Jess came to TOL, she moved into a house with several female roommates, all of whom attended Vanguard Church. They believed in the laying of hands for healing which they could bear witness. She started going to church with them and began to realize that God actually did heal people instantly. She soon realized she had received power and authority through his Holy Spirit to do the same. Whenever she was in need of healing from a headache, back pain or sickness she would ask her roommates to come and pray over her. She was amazed as every time God healed her instantly. She was further amazed when she prayed over her roommates, and they were healed.

She became enthralled with seeing people healed from sickness. She knew she needed to teach the students that God wanted to use them to heal people. Any time someone in her class had a stomachache, headache, pain, or scrape, the kids would pray for one another, and they would be healed.

The kids soon began to learn that they too had power and authority from the Spirit; they were to be like Jesus. They were to do even greater works.

There have been many healing testimonies at Tree of Life. Great things have happened when the children have prayed over people. We give praise to the Father, Son, and Holy Spirit for their supernatural work.

- Talanja once shared that she couldn't drive because she was having seizures. I told her to have the kids pray over her. She hasn't had a seizure since!
- Lance, our board president, told me how his back had been killing him for more than a week. I laid hands on his lower back right there during our lunch meeting. I spoke with him later that day, and he said his back was 100% better!
- Jordan, our amazing music therapy volunteer, came in one morning with a splitting headache. The kids from Jessica's class prayed over her, and it was gone immediately!
- Roger, one of our board members, said he couldn't stand the pain in his hip that had been that way for weeks. I told him to come to worship with me, and we'd have the kids pray over him. After worship I had Roger share his affliction with the kids. They stood up, laid hands on him and commanded the trouble to leave. The next morning he texted me and said he walked a half mile. He was ecstatic that he was completely healed!
- Darcie, one of our parents, limped in one morning with a scowl on her face. She was in obvious pain. She went in with Jessica's kids, and they laid hands on her and prayed for healing to come and the pain to leave in Jesus' name. She walked out much better, and at the end of the day was smiling and said that she was 95% better!
- Jessica had her own testimonies of healing from her class. After returning from Thanksgiving break she shared that she had a headache for a week. She asked us to pray for her. We prayed at the end for the headache to leave in Jesus' name. After we finished, she said she felt as if a hand came from the back of her head and gently pulled the headache away. It was completely gone.

Last year, Jessica showed her class the movie *Finger of God*. In the movie there are many documented miracles and healings and many scenes of gold dust appearing on people. She had experienced "gold dust" from God while worshiping, praying, dancing or just spending time dreaming with Jesus.

After the movie she shared her personal stories. The kids were amazed and excited. They also wanted to experience this. They prayed right then and there and asked Jesus to bless them with a gift that showed His presence. As they sat there with hands open and eyes closed, it happened. The kids looked at their hands. They all had glitter on their hands. Some was gold, some was silver, and some was rainbow-colored. The Bible talks about the glory of the Lord being inside of us. This glitter or gold dust was a manifestation of the glory of God. It became a normal occurrence. During worship or work time, kids would have gold dust or glitter on their hands.

A Seedling - A Chalk Circle
Friday, October 19th, 2012

Alice is a parent who came by TOL to volunteer for the afternoon. I asked her to come with me to put some art supplies into our storage unit downtown. After hauling a few loads into the basement, she said, "Come here a minute, I have something for you." I got a little nervous. She then grabbed a piece of chalk out of the box and drew a four-foot circle on the driveway.

She stood in the circle with hands extended and said come here. She took my hands and began to praise God for Tree of Life and me. It was so powerful and glorious. I told her that she just made my day. It's even more amazing to see where God has brought this woman in such a short time.

Tree of Life also became involved with inner healing and deliverance ministry. We saw many people freed from bondage. Dozens of staff, students, and parents encountered the healing power of Jesus.

Lateesha came to us when she was six years old. She was adopted when she was three and had already experienced a rough beginning. She struggled with Attention Deficit Disorder, and her grandma said she had a lot of trouble in school the previous year. She started off as a first grader at our school, but we quickly learned she was behind academically. When things became too difficult, which was often, she would act out.

One afternoon, Talanja helped remove Lateesha from the classroom because she was being disruptive in a variety of ways. Talanja took her in the multi-purpose room and came to get me for the out-of-control child. When I came in, Lateesha thought it was all quite funny. I firmly told her to come and sit in a chair. She slowly came over and sat. She threatened to spit on me. I raised my eyebrow. She then got out of her chair. I grabbed her, sat her down and held her on my lap. She yelled, "Don't touch me. Get your hands off me!" I told her I would, if she sat in the chair.

She then tried to whack me with the large beads in her hair. She told me to move my head or else she would head-butt me. Since the girl was small, restraint was not an issue. I began to pray. She turned around and looked at me. Where did I see those eyes before? She started to laugh at me. Where did I hear that laugh before?

It began to come back to me. When I was in eighth grade, my friend Chris and I were bored so we made our own Ouija board. I figured this was permissible since the game was sold in the store. We started talking with spirits. Most identified themselves as demons. It was exciting and scary. We were just having fun, right?

Over the course of the next year, we tried a few other forms of channeling spirits. It was very real. It all ended when I was monitoring Chris while he was doing automatic handwriting. The demon, that called himself Legion, took over Chris. He opened his eyes and looked at me. His eyes were evil. Then he started laughing at me. It was pure evil. Although I confessed Jesus as my Lord and Savior, I had no idea what to do. But the Spirit helped me remember the disciples casting out demons. With all my being, I screamed in my mind, "In Jesus' name, demon be gone!" Chris' eyes turned fearful, he let out a gasp and fell limp. He was back to normal. It was surreal, but I knew that I had cast a demon out of my possessed friend.

I had this same sense of an evil spirit possessing Lateesha. I spoke with her mom a few days later, and we decided that Lateesha would repeat kindergarten. The next thing I suggested to mom was that Lateesha go through a deliverance session with Dr. Carr. I explained that he was a gentle Jesus-loving man who had years of experience helping people be set free from generational curses and demonic strongholds. Her mom was in full agreement.

In her new class, Lateesha still had many difficulties with other students. Pamela said that when she played praise music for the class, Lateesha would often ask her to turn it down or she would cover her ears. She was the only student to do this. A few weeks later, Lateesha went through the deliverance session. Her Aunt Melinda was with her as an intercessor. Dr. Carr said he thought it went well. He said that it was harder working with young children because they can't articulate much. They also tended to suppress memories. He encouraged kids to yawn as a physical release to anything spiritually malfeasant. He said there was a lot of deep yawning. Time would tell.

A week later, I asked Pamela how Lateesha was doing. She said, "Oh my goodness, she's a completely different kid! I haven't had one problem with her since. She doesn't cover her ears anymore when we play worship music, and she's been getting along well with her classmates. It's wild." Thank you, God!

A Seedling – Street Ministry
Wednesday, September 26th, 2012 by Jessica

Last Friday the 3rd-5th graders went out on street ministry for the first time this year. Before going out we spent time preparing ourselves by praying over the neighborhood and over specific streets God led us to pray for. We also spent time listening to God about what streets he wanted us to go down and if there was anyone specific we were supposed to look for or pray for.

While out on street ministry, we got to pray for many people and share God's love. A few shining moments for the kids...

- *We prayed God's wisdom over several people, including a group of drug dealers*
- *We prayed for healing for a man with cancer*
- *We prayed for healing for a woman with diabetes*

One of our new students really had a spirit of enthusiasm and boldness. He wanted to be the first one to greet people and say, "Happy Friday! How are you doing today? We are Tree of Life students and going around the neighborhood praying for people. Can we pray for you?"

I am looking forward to the kids bringing and experience God's signs, wonders and miracles in the neighborhood this year!

CHAPTER 18

Being Made New

We praised God for the transformations of those in our school family. And while some of our families were still in hurting positions, some were healing. One of the healing stories is that of Trina.

In May of 2011, I went to the Kalamazoo Gospel Mission to talk to mothers about enrolling their children in our school. I could tell by their body language that most really didn't want to be there. I was some other outsider who thought he had the answer to all of their problems.

When I told them that we charged only 5% of a family's income regardless of the number of kids, they perked up. A mom asked, "What if I have no money?" I told them that the minimum charge was $25 a month. Many were pleasantly surprised. They thought they could actually find a way to come up with the $25 a month. I finished my presentation and talked further with some families.

In July, Vanguard partnered with Stockbridge United Methodist to host the annual summer vacation Bible school. Trina had moved into Edison right around the corner from the church. She had been one of the women who heard me speak at the mission and had brought her boys Eric, Damarquez, and Diontay to the Bible school program. Lance and I were paired up as leaders for a 1st-3rd-grade class. Eric was in our class; he had so many intense questions about God.

By the end of the week Eric had invited Jesus into his heart. We gave him a Bible and got to meet his dad, Shawn. At the end of the week celebration, we had a booth with information and applications to attend our school. Trina was very excited and filled out an application for her boys. I later learned that Nate was actually one of Shawn and Trina's teachers when they attended an alternative high school many years earlier.

On the first day of our second school year we had twenty-nine students, more than double from the previous year. But Eric and Damarquez didn't show up. I went looking for them at their house which was right around the corner from the school. I drove over and knocked on their door. It took a few minutes, but Shawn finally opened the door. It was obvious I had awakened him. I told him that it was the first day of school, I was the principal, and Trina had enrolled them in our school. He seemed unsure but said they would be there tomorrow. This ended up being a somewhat common scenario.

The next day we started school and had worship. The boys weren't there again so I drove over. They were just walking out the door. I picked them up and asked why they were late. They said their mom didn't wake them up. I asked if their mom had an alarm clock. They said she just had her cell phone and sometime she just slept through the alarm. I got them an actual alarm clock.

Over the next several months I built a relationship Trina. She was always very kind and sweet, sometimes even happy when she wasn't stressed and depressed. Sometimes she was high. When I would ask why the boys were late or absent, she would say they were sick or she overslept. She always promised to do better next time.

She would often tell me how excited she was about her boys being at TOL and learning about God. She just loved the school and had even shared about the school with those she waited with at the city bus stop. Although Shawn and Trina had five children together, there were many problems with domestic violence, drugs, joblessness, etc. One of the parents would often leave for weeks or months at a time. Sometimes the children would end up at a relative's house on the east side and therefore couldn't get to school. The home situation was pretty volatile.

I would sometimes go to Trina's house to visit the kids and pray with them. In March, I went over to see how they were doing. She was so depressed and desperate. I cried out to God and told her how much Jesus loved her. When we prayed God was powerful and present.

On March 29, 2011, Trina went to a man's house on the east side to get high. She passed out at some point. When she came to, she was being raped. She grabbed something nearby, stabbed the man, and he died soon after. She was arrested and sent to the county jail. She was 25 years old. We were devastated.

Shawn took the kids and moved to his mom's house on the east side. We had no busing at that time, and Shawn didn't have a car. Sometimes Shawn could get them to school, but when he couldn't I would. Since most of the adults didn't have working phones, it was a crapshoot as to which house they would be at. Furthermore, it was possible that each boy was at a different house on the same morning. Some mornings I would have to drive to multiple houses to find them. Either way, I made sure the kids got to school.

I started visiting Trina at the county jail. This was a whole new experience for me. I honestly never thought I would be doing jail visits as a Christian school principal. I learned you had to go early in the morning and fill out a time request slip to see if the inmate had any visitation slots left for the week. I got an early morning time slot.

When I walked in for the first time, Trina lit up like a Christmas tree! I walked to the booth and looked through the thick wire glass. She signaled me to wait because she had to dial first. She gave me the signal to pick up the phone. I didn't do it right, so she had to do it again. The phone cord was so short that I had to lay my head on my elbow so I could still look at her.

She was so happy. She was clean. She was sober. And she had found Jesus! She told me she was reading her Bible every day, doing the devotions and going to every church service that she could. She knew what she did was wrong and there was a price to pay. She had decided to take a plea bargain for a five to seven year sentence in lieu of a trial that could lead to a life sentence. She missed her children dearly. We prayed. I walked out encouraged and uplifted.

Summer came and went. Our third year at Tree of Life began. We were in our new building now. I noticed right away that Eric and Damarquez did not show. I found out Shawn had moved to an apartment that was outside our busing district. Trina was crushed.

I went to visit Trina the day before she was transferred to the state penitentiary in Ypsilanti. As I walked into the phone room, she was smiling and waving to me. I thought to myself, *this does not look like a woman who has been given seven years for murder.* But, as I talked with her, it became obvious that although her body was in prison, her spirit was free in Christ.

She again told me how she could see Him all throughout her life. She saw Jesus in the street minister, Nate, years ago when she was a student. She even knew Jesus was there the night before the murder when she said she heard a voice say, *"Don't go. Don't go."* She told me that every time she talked to her mom and family she would stress how important it was that they get to know Jesus. She told me how God was going to take care of her.

"I know God's got me, but I have one request, Mr. S. If there's anything you can do to get my kids back at Tree of Life, that would be amazing," she pleaded.

This was her last request. This was her prayer and I was taken aback. After we prayed, I encouraged her that God was writing one heck of a story with her. Instead of walking out discouraged, I walked out completely encouraged. I called Shawn and asked him if I got the kids rides to and from school, would he send them back? He agreed. I wrote a letter to the TOL family asking for help with rides. Between the boy's family, the TOL family and a bunch of interns from Bethany Christian services, we were able to get them transportation for every day of the week.

It was so great to have Eric and Damarquez back. But after Christmas break the boys didn't return. Shawn said that arranging rides was just too much, and they would have to go back to the public school in their district. Our hearts were heavy.

I was able to stay in contact with Trina by emailing her through jpay.com, which is a prison e-mail system. Her letters have been such an encouragement.

Mr. S

How are you? I want to say Merry Christmas and Happy New Year. Also thank you for everything that you do. I know that it is our heavenly Father and every good gift is always from the Him. I only have 15 minutes on the j pay. I would love to hear from the kids I talked to them the other day it was cool. Damarquez is not ok I hear it in his voice. I hope when the visits come that I can help. Also I excited about a program thru the chaplain called Moms in touch program. I'm in a level 4– 22-hour lockdown, so not much I can do back here. I should only be here not long still ticket free ☺ I'm trying to get into everything and I know Phil. 4:13 all-day. Thank you and God bless. 12/17/2012

Like any technology or social media, it can be used for good or evil. It seems like most people either love or hate Facebook. I opened an account in 2010, "friended" everyone I could and used it to promote what God was doing at TOL. In fact, we shared more pictures and stories on Facebook than any e-mail or traditional mailings.

In April of 2011, we tried a Facebook experiment. We were in need of $30,000 for the remainder of our annual budget. At the time, I had 1,500 friends on my Facebook page. I realized that if each one of them donated $20 to the kids at TOL, our budget for the remainder of the year would be met. So, I posted the following challenge:

When does 20 = 30,000?

What can you get for $20? You can buy 20 songs on iTunes, half a tank of gas, or dinner for 2 at Chili's. You can play nine holes, get two movie tickets and small popcorn, or two t-shirts on spring break. Or, you can have an eternal impact on a child's life. http://tolschool.org/donate/

I posted this on my Facebook page several times for one week. The response was great. Although we did not receive $30,000, we praised God for the $3,000 that came in a week.

Many of our TOL families had need for an alarm clock. Maybe they didn't own one or their cell phone just wasn't cutting it. I was in the office one day asking a student why he was late to school again. His family overslept and no one woke him up. I asked, "Are you old enough to use an alarm clock?" He replied yes so I said I would get him one.

A little later, I posted on Facebook that we were in need of alarm clocks to hand out to our families. An hour later a guy I had never met walked in with a bag of alarm clocks. He said his wife saw the post on Facebook and sent him to bring them to TOL. Talanja and I were blown away and praised God for such an immediate answer to prayer.

In January of 2013, Amy and I were blessed with a three-night vacation in Traverse City. I was checking my e-mail in our hotel room, and I yelled for Amy to come check this out. We had received an online donation for $5,000! What made it even more incredible is that I had never talked to this person, emailed her anything, nor mailed her anything about TOL. I did notice that I was "friends" with her daughter on Facebook.

In November of 2012, I met Xavier's mom, Betty. She was a public school bus driver. Her son was in second grade at another school, and things were not going well. Xavier was the youngest of Betty's five adopted children. They all had special needs, except for Xavier, and she wanted to keep it that way. She knew Xavier was very smart but had some behavioral issues. She began to tell me in detail about how he would tear apart classrooms, yell at teachers, and run away from school. I thought, *"Dear Jesus! Do I want this at our school? It has been so peaceful."* But I heard the Spirit nudging me to accept him. After praying and talking about it with his teacher, we accepted him.

The first couple of days went great. We were pleased. He was super sweet and gave us hugs. We knew that sometimes kids just needed a different environment, and many issues would work themselves out. Then the third day came. I left school to go downtown to pick up some miscellaneous office supplies that a company was donating. I stepped in the elevator to return and my wife called. "You better get back to school." It was Xavier. My heart sank.

When I pulled up to school, Xavier's entire class was outside. They saw me pull up and came running and screaming towards the car. I yelled back at them, "NO! We're not going to act like that." I went in and saw the look on everybody's faces. Xavier was calming down in a hallway chair.

I looked in Annie's classroom. Several people were picking up what was the result of what looked like a tornado had come through. Books were strewn everywhere, shelves and chairs were toppled, pens and pencils were scattered like pick-up sticks. Annie reported the only thing truly broken was her set of chimes. I asked if everyone was okay; they all were a bit shaken, but okay.

Annie recounted the incident. Xavier started getting angry and hid under the table. She thought it best to let him ride it out. Suddenly he came out from under the table and went ballistic. She had everyone else leave the classroom and left him alone since she was unable to subdue him. After a few minutes, he ran out the fire exit and away from school. Our lunch helper, Terry, chased after him. He eventually caught him and hauled him back to school over his shoulder. This was the start of an amazing and difficult journey for us all.

Xavier was adopted when he was three. He must have gone through some absolutely horrible experiences before Betty adopted him. He was on seven different medications, walked hunched over and looked angry. He had a large tumor removed from the back of his neck when he was four. Betty loved him dearly but pulled no punches. She wanted the best for him and didn't want him labeled. When she came to us, she was hoping that we could fix things.

Xavier was one of the sweetest kids I'd ever known. He would come in everyday and give me a hug. He had the biggest smile. He had a soft voice with a little lisp. He loved reading and mathematics. He was good 95% of the day. But when he "went to his dangerous place," he would turn into a complete monster. You could not reason with him. He would simply rage.

We prayed and prayed. We tried everything. We changed every variable under the sun. We tried positive reinforcement. We talked with social workers, read stuff on the Internet. He even went through a Deliverance session with Dr. Carr. Although I believe anything evil that was clinging to him was now gone, his brain wasn't healed. All we figured out was that there was no rhyme or reason to when he would erupt. I was resolved to making sure he never destroyed another classroom. Since I was the only one who could physically remove him, I was on call every minute of every day.

There were so many occasions with Xavier that, by February I became suddenly depressed. I asked prayer warriors to pray for me. The Spirit made it clear that I was under attack. The enemy was sowing lies into my mind: *This kind of thing shouldn't be happening at a Christian school. If you really knew what you were doing, this wouldn't be happening. There are others far more qualified to help him. You just want to get rid of him, don't you?*

I was so thankful for praying friends because within a day, the lies were revealed, and I rebuked them. I claimed God's truth. We loved Xavier dearly. We were going to keep serving him the best we could. My dad reminded me, "You've got an army behind you." My friend Esto told me, "Where else would this boy receive this kind of love? This is exactly where he needs to be."

Things started to get worse at home, and Betty decided that Xavier needed a full psychological evaluation. When the results came back, it was no surprise that he was labeled with post-traumatic stress syndrome. It all made sense. The psychiatrist changed some of his meds, and after spring break Xavier stopped running away from school. He still went to his dangerous place at times, but his biggest victory was not running from school anymore.

We started asking ourselves if we could continue to effectively serve him through the rest of the year. I talked with Annie and made sure that she and the other students were up to the challenge. She reiterated that as long as she could count on me for removing him, she would be all right. Then things began to change.

I was out playing catch with Daydrianna one day at recess when I asked her who taught her to throw so well. She said Xavier.

One day a kindergartner named Denivion walked in from recess with a bloody nose. Xavier happened to be passing through in the hallway. He quickly went over and put his arm around her. "Are you okay?" She nodded and he continued to walk with his arm around her back towards her classroom. As he walked away from her he said, "I'm going to pray that Jesus heals your nose." I was shocked and overjoyed.

Our music teacher Brittany asked me one day if Xavier would like a private piano lesson. I told her that would be awesome so she did. After the lesson, Brittany reported how Xavier loved it. He caught on so quickly—faster than many of the older kids. Xavier asked her, "Are there a lot of patterns in music?" Brilliant!

Later I asked Betty if she would like to take the school keyboard home for Xavier to keep. It was donated, but I believed God wanted him to have it. I had confirmation, because the next day someone donated a high quality digital piano. Go, Jesus!

In Xavier's last week of school, he came in the office one day and said he wanted to write me a note. He wrote intensely for several minutes. "Have an awesome day. Today I am still working on it. I'm going to keep trying to pray for and love everybody by acting like Lord Jesus! I'm still working on it. We're going to win! Forever and ever, the party [in Heaven] will never end."

I'm convinced that God will use Xavier to change the world!

A Seedling - Best Donation Ever
April 2013

Last week, I got a check in the mail for $10. I cried.

The check came from the Huron Valley Correctional Valley Institution in Ypsilanti where Trina was serving her time in prison.

> *Hey Mr. S,*
>
> *Glory to God as I continue in this joyous struggle. It's not me but Him who lives in me. I am taking every day as is. I miss my children a lot but its ok cause in chapter 42 of Job (I believe) He says I will be blessed more in the later than in the beginning. I appreciate so much. You all do and have done so much not only for my children, but the whole community. I also have a job and I choose to bless as He blesses me.*
>
> *Trina*

God is so good! I have been so encouraged by Trina that it's hard to put into words. I know that when I received this monetary seed that it was a sign from God that the Tree of Life expansion is on its way!

***

My life changed again when I met Lucy back in 2010. It was an amazing story how we met and how she enrolled her kids at our school right on the hood of my car. She loved her children and tried the best she could. She had been labeled bipolar. At age 28, she had seven children.

When we had met, they were living at her boyfriend's father's place. There were so many people coming and going, and eventually, Lucy's dad, a retired veteran, started living with them as well. One of the first tragedies that we experienced with Lucy was when her brother, Alan, committed suicide at age 26. Lucy and the older girls were devastated. He was their favorite uncle. I was glad we were able to be there to support the family with love, comfort and prayer.

Lucy dropped off the kids at school one day with her dad. She was an emotional wreck. I told her that I would stop by later. When I arrived at her house, it was a mess. She was going on and on about her pain and troubles. She told me sobbing, "I just can't do it, Mr. S. I just can't take it anymore."

I urgently told her that there is a better way. I told her Jesus is the only one who can help you out of any of the messes that she kept finding herself in. She was willing, so we prayed for her to receive Christ. Another day, she asked if she could talk to me. In a begrudging manner she told me she was pregnant with her seventh child. I was angry at first, but I held my tongue and asked, "You do know how this happens, don't you?" Since she constantly complained about what a hassle her kids were, I strongly suggested that she get her tubes tied.

I often asked myself why people in poverty had so many kids. I knew some people believed it was for more government money. I wondered if it was the beauty of creating life. I wondered if for some people it was the only thing that gave them worth. I wondered if for some, creating life was the only thing they ever felt they did worthwhile in their life.

Lucy's dad's health started to deteriorate. He wound up getting his own house on the North side of Kalamazoo. Lucy had the three oldest kids live with her boyfriend's father, and the three youngest stayed with their dad. She would often have to take trips to the Veteran's Administration Hospital in Ann Arbor and take her 9-year-old daughter for moral support.

One night Lucy's brother came over to grandpa's house with a friend. They decided they would try and cook up some meth in the basement while everyone was sleeping. The meth lab blew up. Everyone made it out safely except for Lucy's brother who was badly burned. The house and its entire contents were immediately condemned. Lucy and her kids lost everything.

I spent the first part of summer break helping Lucy's family relocate, attain new clothes and get food. The TOL family was so helpful and supportive. Within a month, the Lord provided her with her own place just a few blocks down the street from us. She was so happy, proud and extremely grateful.

Just over a month later, her dad, who was her rock and main support, passed away. She spiraled into depression. Again, the TOL family helped her with the funeral arrangements and many other things. Lucy was an emotional decision maker. It didn't bode well in any situation, but it was especially bad when it came to personal finances. We always tried to help her get out of the next bind. Praise God, she eventually appointed a third party to oversee her income and bills.

One time she got so mad at her kids for not listening to her, she actually pulled them out of TOL and sent them to public school for two days. I strongly discouraged her, but she did it anyway. I know that she often felt so helpless that to her, doing something was better than doing nothing.

Before the start of the third TOL school year, I had contacted Lucy to make sure the kids were still coming back. She was excited and absolutely positive. A week later that changed, and she put them in public school for the entire third year. We praised God that the mentors who had come alongside the kids and her family were still going strong. The TOL family has helped Lucy's family buy cars, provide overnight childcare, get clothes, furniture, diapers, food, money, gas, repairs, nitpick lice and so much more.

But before our fourth year, Lucy stopped by my house and asked if her children could come back. We still had room, and we knew that they should still be at TOL. I had her fill out another enrollment application which she turned in right away.

A Seedling - More Fruit
June 2013

A couple of months after I received a donation from Trina, another envelope from the same prison came into our office. I was stunned to see another love offering to the Lord. However, I almost became lightheaded with joy and wonder when I found the following note enclosed with a check from another inmate:

> *Not so long ago I had the great pleasure of meeting Trina. She has been my inspiration in giving my life back to Christ. I've gotten back in church and have been doing a lot of spiritual reading. In doing so, the subject of tithing keeps coming up. I have been feeling compelled to do so, but have no church or organization that I know of to send such tithes. I talked to Trina about it one day and over the next couple of days it came to mind that Trina tithes to her children's school. So I asked her if I could give her the money to tithe this month. Graciously she said no thank you, but you can send it to them directly. So please accept this small offering on behalf of my friend, Trina. She speaks so highly of your school and what you have done for her family.*

> *Thank You,*

> *Ginger*

> *#123456*

> *Ypsilanti Women's Correctional Facility*

In the first week of June 2013, we took the 3rd-5th-grade class to Forefront shelter in Benton Harbor for a field trip. It's so amazing to watch the kids be totally comfortable around so many tough characters that were smoking, drinking, dealing and cursing. They got right into handing out waters to everybody. Another group of kids prepared the meal for house church. They lifted up the day in prayer during our prayer time and gave words of encouragement to those who came for prayer. One man with severe back pain was prayed over by the kid and was healed! Several kids said this was the best field trip of the year. A couple of the students even drove back with Jessica over the summer to go minister.

A Seedling - Double or Nothing

TOL Student Reading Improvement Data

2012-2013

At Tree of Life we use <u>Scholastic A-Z Reading Assessments</u>. The following data is based on those reading assessments.

The line on each graph shows where students should be reading by the end of the year for that grade. This year we had no 3rd graders.

The most significant statistic that can be gathered here is that **on average every student at TOL more than doubled their reading ability level in one school year!**

TOL Quick Facts 2013

- 51 Students in grades PreK-5. Over 20 students were turned away due to limited space.
- 75% of students are minorities
- One principal, three teachers, part time music teacher, PE teacher, art teacher, music/speech/behavior therapist, Title 1 teacher, and many, many volunteers
- 2nd year in new 5,000 square foot first class facility.
- $180,000 annual budget. 90% met by donations. 10% met by parent's tuition.
- 50% of TOL families have a single mom as head of the household
- 75% of TOL families are on some form of government assistance
- 75% live or have lived in the Edison Neighborhood
- 50% of TOL kids have little or no church connection
- $18,000 average income for TOL families
- Verse of the Year – "Jesus looked at them intently and said, 'Humanly speaking, it is impossible. But with God everything is possible.'" Matthew 19:26

CHAPTER 19

Reproducing Fruit

Things had begun to change for Tree of Life School. After making it through a major building project and focusing on the needs of our students and their families, God began to call for us to stretch beyond Kalamazoo.

Jessica had heard the call to start an urban Christian school years ago before she even became a teacher. It had become clear at this point that Jessica was to be the principal at the new sister school we were planting in Benton Harbor, Michigan. This city was even more urban and impoverished than the Edison Neighborhood. Knowing that she was leaving us, we prayed intently for the Lord to provide her replacement at Tree of Life, someone as good or better.

We were honored and humbled to have ten applicants apply for her position. One potential teacher named Becky stopped by the school to personally drop off her application. It was obvious that she was very excited about joining our staff. I asked her how she heard about us, and she told me that she had been working with preschool children at Head Start for seven years. One day she was unexpectedly informed that she would be going on a field trip with the kids.

She wasn't terribly excited since that meant a nine-hour day with no breaks from the kids. They got loaded on the short bus and headed out. They happen to drive by the construction site for the new TOL building. Becky was stunned to see it. She thought she knew of every school in the area. She googled it and checked out our website. She fell in love with what God was doing at TOL and said she nearly flipped out when she saw the job posting. She thought it couldn't be true and called to double check. She also knew that she was going to lose her job at Head Start at the end of the year because of budget cuts, so she was already looking for a new job.

As she shared her story with me in the hallway, a student named Deairra walked out of her classroom to use the restroom. Becky whispered to me excitedly, "Oh my goodness, that's one of my former preschool students!" I encouraged her to go say hello and give her a hug. It was a tender moment. Becky then told me that she would pray over each one of her students each and every day. Not out loud, because that was unlawful. Silently she would pray intently over each child. She prayed that they would find Jesus and His plan for their life. I was deeply moved by her testimony. A few months and a couple of interviews later we hired Becky. There is no question that she is exactly who we needed and that she needed us. That's the Kingdom.

Jenna had been a student for two years at Tree of Life. She grew by leaps and bounds spiritually and academically. Jerry and I had been talking for quite some time about finding a way for our students to go to Heritage Christian Academy. Between Jerry, God and me, we all felt that kids from our school should have the opportunity to continue in Christian education if they felt called.

I talked with Jenna's parents, Josh and Sarah, about future educational plans. They really felt that Jenna should continue in a Christian School but didn't know how they could ever afford it. We moved forward in faith. Three weeks before the start of school I called Sarah and told her to just go start the enrollment process at HCA for Jenna. I then posted the following story on August 25, 2013.

> *I can't tell you the number of times people have asked me, "So what happens when kids finish at TOL?" My response has always been, "I don't know, but we're praying into it." Over the past year some things have become clear. First, God wants kids who finish at TOL to have an option to continue at a Christian school with a similar cost structure if they so*

choose. Second, the Lord has opened our first door with our partners at Heritage Christian Academy.

I met Jenna's mom and stepdad at the mission two years ago. They had moved out of their home and checked the whole family of six into the Family Life Program because they knew they had a drug problem, and they knew they needed to become more intimate with the Lord.

Jenna grew by leaps and bounds in her relationship with the Lord as well as in her academics. She was a true leader in her class and the school. She's been a powerful force as we did street ministry in the neighborhood. She loved doing ministry at the Forefront House in Benton Harbor.

The other element that is clear to both her parents and to me is that she needs to continue in Christian education. With Jenna's parents portion and tuition assistance available through HCA, their remaining need for Jenna's 7th grade year is $3,800 or $1900 for the first semester. We at TOL are so convicted of this that TOL is going to donate the first $500. That means our immediate need is now $1,400.

If you feel led by the Spirit to donate towards Jenna and other Tree of Life students continuing in Christian education, please write your tax-deductible donation to Heritage Christian Academy. Simply write TOLTAF (Tree of Life Tuition Assistance Fund) on the memo. Send checks to 6312 Quail Run Dr. 49009.

We prayed. Seven days later I received notification from HCA. People had donated $3,800. I cried and thanked Jesus profusely. A week or so later I posted an email from Sarah.

Praise God! Adam, I can't explain what this is doing not just for my faith, but for Jenna's.

*I know that sometimes God closes a door to us and sometimes
His answer is "No," but I clearly see that God is using others
to fulfill His will in Jenna's life, and that He is saying, "Yes."
He does support our decision in sending her to Heritage!*

*I'm telling you, Adam, Jenna is seeing God work in a way
she never has before. Will you please tell everyone "Thank
you" from us? Just let people know that Jenna's parents are
truly grateful!*

***

Nate and Jessica were a part of the same house church in Kalamazoo. During our first year at TOL, Nate had also mentioned something similar to Jessica about starting a school in Benton Harbor. She had been feeling for a little while that she needed to start spending time in Benton Harbor. In the summer of 2011, she started going with Nate on Wednesday's to help at the Forefront ministry house. She quickly grew to love the city of Benton Harbor and its people because it reminded her of Detroit.

Jessica went to college in the metro Detroit area. As a photographer, she spent a great deal of time in the inner city capturing images of the community and its people. This led to innumerable opportunities to talk to people on the streets and hear their stories. She quickly fell in love with Detroit and its people. Before graduating she prayed to God, "I want you to send me somewhere where I can live, work, and worship all in the same neighborhood. A place like Detroit."

After accepting the position at Tree of Life in 2010, she thought this fulfilled the call from God to start an urban Christian school. Little did she realize this was just the beginning. In her first year of teaching at TOL, she began researching Masters level programs for curriculum and development. The more she researched, the more she sensed from the Lord that she was to pursue a program in educational leadership. This became clearer after a friend challenged her to really listen to what God was asking her to do. Jessica "played it safe" and took a class that would count towards either program.

On a Wednesday during Christmas break in 2011, Jessica, Roger and I went to Forefront. During prayer we asked God whether or not he wanted another school like ours in Benton Harbor. After prayer we all felt God lay a definite 'yes' on our hearts. We also knew that people would think us crazy to start another school so soon. But then again, Tree of Life was a crazy enough story, so why not another? We got excited about what God was asking us to do. We drove around Benton Harbor with Tokyo, a Benton Harbor native, as our tour guide. He showed us all the vacant elementary schools that we could potentially use. As we were driving, God highlighted one of the buildings to Jessica, and she felt convicted that was where the new school should be.

She continued to argue with God about why she couldn't start a school or be a principal. She felt she was too young. She felt that no one would ever trust her. Her only experience was teaching in the classroom for two years. She was a small white girl in a predominately black, male dominated community. She was an outsider. She didn't have credentials people might expect for the position. Despite her excitement and confidence for the new school, she felt unqualified to be the principal.

Over spring break we went back to Forefront and prayed specifically about the name of the school. While praying we heard the name River of Life. Benton Harbor has a twin city called, St. Joseph. The St. Joseph River divides the cities both racially and economically. St. Joseph is 90% white; Benton Harbor is 90% black. St. Joseph has a median income of $65,000 and Benton Harbor's median income is $18,000. We felt River Of Life was to be an essential part of reconciling that divide. Later that day we went back to the building Jessica had heard from God about. We put a stake in that ground claiming that location as the future site of River Of Life.

Also during our prayer time, we cried out to God to raise a champion for this new school. Little did we know it would be Jessica. Although she was too scared to share with us at that time, she knew in the back of her mind that we were praying for her. She knew that whoever championed this school had to fully understand what God had already done at TOL.

Later in the summer of 2012, Jessica went to a prophetic conference in Michigan. Someone who knew nothing about this new school came to her with a word from God. "God said there is something He keeps asking you to do and you keep telling him no. And He wants you to go talk to Him about it and listen to what He has to say." Instantly, she was struck with fear. She knew exactly that this word was about River Of Life.

Instead, she went to talk to a friend first. She told her to go talk to God. Jessica then presented every question and excuse to God about this calling. He gently gave an answer to every question. He gave a response to every excuse. She was filled with awe and terror. She wept like she never did before.

The next day Jessica shared with me everything God had told her. I was sad for a minute, but then quickly realized what God was up to. My sadness turned to joy. I affirmed Jessica in her calling as the principal at River Of Life. She later shared the same with Nate. Nate let her know that he had already heard this in his prayer time a week earlier.

We pursued the Benton Harbor Area School building for nine months. They eventually declined our partnership offer. We sought other buildings. Jessica met Lisa the director at Lighthouse Ministries. Although they didn't hit it off right away, the Spirit brought them together. Lighthouse was housed in a Methodist church that was over one hundred years old. In the 1950's they added on a two-story classroom building. River of Life would rent classrooms located on the second floor. Sound familiar?

My son Isaac, a student of Jessica's for four years, always drew a picture of a lighthouse when asked to draw what God was showing him. Jessica always wondered why he drew the same thing. She even became irritated by it. We eventually discerned that ROL was to be housed at Lighthouse Ministries. Months later, Jessica realized that as soon we did, Isaac stopped drawing lighthouses.

Lighthouse ministries started the same year as TOL in the heart of Benton Harbor. The executive director, Lisa, was a native of Benton Harbor. She had been living in Atlanta, but God called her back. Her heart was on fire for the children. Lighthouse Ministries was a place for children to be tutored, mentored, and go to summer camp. They provided services for children before and after school and during the summer. But something was missing. The directors were praying for someone to come alongside them for over three years.

River Of Life opened its doors September of 2014 in the Lighthouse Ministry Center. Jessica taught fulltime grades three through five and was the principal. Liz taught grades Kindergarten through two. They had a budget of $75,000 for the year. They had $5,000 to start. And you'll never guess how many kids showed up the first day. Twelve. All glory to God!

At least a year before we opened the doors at Tree of Life, my family was at Vanguard worshipping. I was agonizing in silent prayer over the seemingly impossible things that had transpired over the last few years. I remember someone sitting behind me putting hands on my shoulder. It was Natalee. She spoke a prophetic word to me. "God is having you go through all of this, but it's not just for Tree of Life. Tree of Life is going to be the first of many." I was overcome.

With Jessica launching River of Life, this prophetic Word has been affirmed. The move was bittersweet. In addition to Jessica moving on, Pamela would be heading back to the Winnipeg, Canada to be with her husband who had a job there. Maybe she will start a school there?

Jessica keeps bugging me about setting up a non-profit for Schools Of Life so that we can start these schools up even faster all over the world. One thing at a time, Jessica! We're praying into it. Whatever you want, Lord.

AFTERWORD

A Seedling - The Expansion
March 2013

Praise God for all He is doing in and through the TOL Family. We are so thankful for the amazing 40 kids in PreK-5th grade this year. We are so thankful for our first year in our brand new facility that is state-of-the-art, energy efficient, first class, and debt free!

One parent wrote this about TOL this year:

"Tree of Life has been such a blessing, mainly because it is the only beacon of light in my life as well as my daughter's. I am not living up to my full potential where Christ is concerned. So to have people who love God and are willing to help show my daughter what salvation is and how to walk in it is so important to me. Yes, it has been a sacrifice keeping her there as opposed to KPS, but I refuse to let the enemy trick me out of being a part of what God is doing at Tree of Life. Keep up the good work, TOL family."

What has become clear is that the Lord wants to increase the number of students and families that become a part of TOL. In the fall, we anticipate having 60 students in PreK-5th grade. And though we are excited, we have determined that 60 students is the maximum number of students that we can love and serve with excellence in our existing 5,000-square-foot facility. In the fall, we will start the waiting list and begin to turn people away.

In seeking the desires of the Lord, we have discerned that he would like to triple the number of students to 180 and serve grades PreK-8th grade. In order to do this, we need to add an additional eight classrooms, more office space, special pullout rooms, lunchroom, and a community gym. This will require additional land and approximately 2.5 million dollars.

We know that if we have heard the Lord correctly, He will see it done! 1 John 5:14-15 proclaims, "And we are confident that He hears us whenever we ask for anything that pleases Him. And since we know He hears us when we make our requests, we also know that He will give us what we ask for." Our faith has been greatly increased. We have watched Him build a brand new $800,000 facility with no debt or loans in less than two years.

We humbly ask for your prayers and support as we pursue God in building this significant expansion that will impact the Edison neighborhood for generations to come.

Glory to God!

TREE OF LIFE EXPANSION PROJECT

- *Serving 180 Students in K – 8th Grade*

- *8 Additional Classrooms, Lunch Room, More Offices, Pull Out Rooms*

- *Full Size Community Gym serving hundreds more community youth after school and weekends*

- *Estimated Cost: $2.5 Million*

- *Time Frame: Opening Fall of 2016*

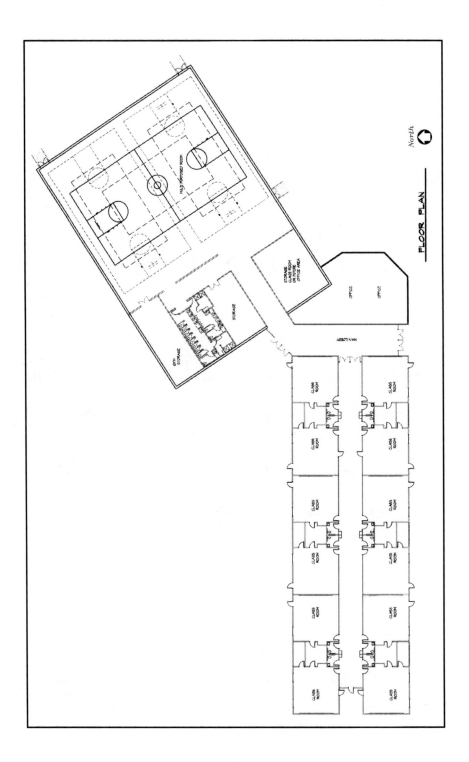

North

FLOOR PLAN

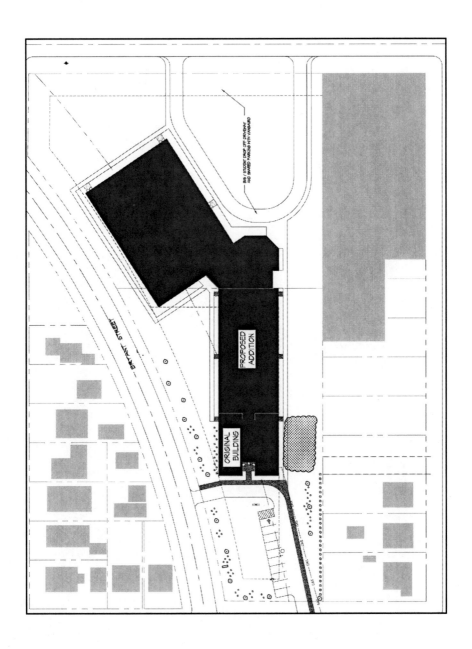

CPSIA information can be obtained at www.ICGtesting.com
Printed in the USA
LVOW08s0706310715

448275LV00002B/2/P